Shaped by God

Twelve Essentials for Nurturing Faith in Children, Youth, and Adults

Edited by Robert J. Keeley

FAITH
ALIVE®
Christian Resources

Grand Rapids, Michigan

We welcome your comments. Call us at 1-800-333-8300, or email us at editors@faithaliveresources.org.

Library of Congress Cataloging-in-Publication Data
Shaped by God: twelve essentials for nurturing faith in children, youth, and adults / edited by Robert J. Keeley.
    p. cm.
Includes bibliographical references.
ISBN 978-1-59255-490-4
1. Spiritual formation—Christian Reformed Church. I. Keeley, Robert J., 1954-
BV4511.S55 2010   2010012806
253.5—dc22

FSC
Mixed Sources
Product group from well-managed
forests, controlled sources and
recycled wood or fiber

Cert no. SCS-COC-002464
www.fsc.org
©1996 Forest Stewardship Council

10 9 8 7 6 5 4 3 2 1

Contents

Foreword *Timothy Brown* 5

Introduction *Robert J. Keeley* 7

1   Wide and Long and High and Deep: Biblical Foundations
of Faith Formation *Syd Hielema* 9

2   Embodied Wisdom: Faith Formation through
Faith Practices *Don C. Richter* 23

3   Distinguishing Dragons: The Importance of Story
in Faith Formation *Sarah Arthur*. 37

4   "It's What We Do": Faith Formation at Home
Elizabeth F. Caldwell 47

5   Step By Step: Faith Development and Faith Formation
Robert J. Keeley. 59

6   Liturgy for a Lifetime: Faith Formation through Worship
Robbie Fox Castleman 71

7   Living Mysteries: Sacraments and the Education
of Christians *Fred P. Edie* 81

8   Beyond the Schooling Model: Faith Formation in the
Educational Context *Marian R. Plant*. 97

9   No Better Place: Fostering Intergenerational Christian
Community *Holly Catterton Allen* 109

10 Exchanging Gifts: Faith Formation and People with
Developmental Disabilities *Erik W. Carter* 127

11 Growing in Wisdom and Stature: Recent Research on
Spirituality and Faith Formation *Kevin E. Lawson* 139

12 Questioning the "Right" Answers: Faith Formation in
the Postmodern Matrix *David M. Csinos*. 153

Conclusion: The People of the Story of God's Faithfulness
Robert J. Keeley. 165

Contributors 169

Endnotes 173

Foreword

A long time ago, in the early years of the twelfth century, just when the human race was beginning to scratch and claw its way out of the Dark Ages, a Cistercian preacher named Alan of Lille wrote a book. While it bore the cumbersome and uninviting title *Compendium*, every page rippled with meaning—and quite frankly ripples still. It is one of a handful of books that I treasure most. Though Alan was writing mostly to preachers, his pulsing passion for every Christian to "climb Jacob's ladder" made it, and makes it still, a must-read for everyone.

"Jacob's ladder" was a controlling metaphor for Alan. He imagined a seven-rung ladder mounted on earth and reaching into heaven. Each ascending rung marked still another step in attaining spiritual maturity. The first rung, as you might expect, was a sinner's confession of sins. The second rung was a prayer for forgiving grace; and the third, the proper gratitude owed the Holy One for grace received. The fourth rung was a careful reading of Holy Scripture; and the fifth, inquiring of a more mature brother or sister concerning those parts of Scripture that were difficult to understand. The sixth rung was becoming a mentor for a brother or sister who needs assistance. The final rung was attained when the developing Christian muscled up the courage to proclaim publicly the faith he or she had acquired through the Word.

This language may seem as quaint and curious as the doilies in your grandmother's living room, but that is more a commentary on us than it is on Alan of Lille. Growing up and becoming fully mature and faithful followers of Jesus Christ is of critical concern to the whole church. As I write this foreword, I am holding in my hand the December 10, 2009, edition of *USA Today*. The headline, "Mixing Their Religion: Many Choose Their Faith from a Spiritual Buffet," underlines the timeliness of this book. The article goes on to outline the stunning capacity of self-identified American Christians to pick and choose their favorite religious convictions and practices from a long list of religions and to fashion a new one for themselves. If you find reports like this alarming, as I do, this volume is for you.

As the apostle Paul cautioned our sisters and brothers in the world city of Ephesus, "We must no longer be children, tossed to and fro and blown about by every wind of doctrine, by people's trickery, by their craftiness in deceitful scheming" (Eph. 4:14).

My wife, Nancy, and I have three married children and nine grandchildren. We pray for them every day by name, often through our tears. We want to grow old knowing that they all walk in the truth. If ever following Jesus and growing into full maturity in him was easy, it certainly isn't now. This book will help you and those whom you love in this most critical concern for every Christian.

The *Compendium* concludes with a really interesting sermon once preached by Alan of Lille titled *Ad Somnolentes.* Just in case your Latin is a little rusty, that means, "To Sleepyheads." If you or some of the people you love have become spiritual sleepyheads, this lovely compilation on spiritual formation is just the wake-up call you need. Read it and awaken to a world of possibilities! And then pass it along as quickly as you can.

Timothy Brown
December 2009

Introduction

I don't remember a time when I didn't know about God. I was raised in a home where prayer, attending worship, and Bible reading were always present. It was just the way things were. That formed the foundation for my faith, and my faith continued to grow even after I left my parents' home. People and events had an impact on my faith development over the years. I can think of family members, teachers (both at church and in school), youth leaders, pastors, friends, and colleagues who have played an important role in forming my faith. The list doesn't just include people from the past, of course—my faith is still being nurtured and is still developing even now.

There are a lot of people like me—people who grew up in a faith-nurturing environment. But many others came to know the Lord later in life. Their story of faith might be more like the prodigal son or like the apostle Paul, who met the Lord in a flash on the road to Damascus. As we talk to each other about our faith stories, we see that God has brought each of us to faith in different ways. Nurturing faith, then, is not a one-size-fits-all proposition. There are many facets to growing faith in children and adults.

This book celebrates those different facets. In the chapters that follow you will hear from some of the best thinkers in the field of faith nurture. They represent a broad range of expertise from across the Christian community and across North America. As you read these pages, you'll discover the growing consensus of what effective faith nurture looks like. You'll note that each author speaks with his or her own particular voice and from his or her own particular theological background. They don't speak with one voice, but they are all voices in the same chorus.

You'll need to adapt some of the ideas you read in this book to fit your own church or denomination. It is our hope that you will see new opportunities to strengthen your ministry in ways that all the members of your congregation, young and old, can grow closer to God.

I am grateful to a number of people who were helpful in the development of this book.

- The team at Faith Alive, particularly Leonard Vander Zee, Ruth VanderHart, Jolanda Howe, and Lynn Setsma.

- John Witvliet and the staff at the Calvin Institute of Christian Worship. I am blessed to be able to continue working with this fine group.

- The faculty, administration, staff, and students of Calvin College, especially my friends and colleagues in the Education Department.

- The contributors to this book, many of whom were helpful in introducing me to others who became contributors. All of them were wonderful. Thanks for your fine work on this project.

- My children, Bethany, Meredith, Bryan, and Lynnae, who are now leaders in their own churches and help me to think about faith nurture in new ways.

- My wife, Laura, who in addition to being on the editorial committee for this book is and has been my best friend and partner in ministry for over thirty years.

Robert J. Keeley
January 2010

Chapter 1

Wide and Long and High and Deep:

Biblical Foundations of Faith Formation

Syd Hielema

Ask ten people to sketch out the story of their walk with God—the story of their faith formation—and you will hear ten very different stories. Search the Bible for a systematic program on which to base faith formation strategies in the church, home, or school, and you'll be searching for a long time. But look for common threads in those stories and in Scripture, and you will find them.

In this chapter we'll discern and describe some of those common threads. As you read, I invite you to ask yourself two questions: "To what extent do these threads resonate with my reading of the Scriptures and the faith stories I'm familiar with?" and "To what extent do the faith formation practices in our church, home, or school embody these threads?" With these two questions in mind, this chapter aims to refocus teachers and parents in their callings to faith formation or to serve as a discussion guide for church or school teams as they begin another season.

We'll look at two Scripture passages, Ephesians 3:14-21 and Deuteronomy 6:4-9, and distill from them nine themes that describe the character and activity of faith formation. Some commentators refer to Ephesians as the jewel in the crown of Paul's writings because it celebrates the wonder and majesty of Jesus in such a profound yet concise manner. At the center of this letter (3:14-21) we find this intense prayer:

> For this reason I kneel before the Father, from whom every family in heaven and on earth derives its name. I pray that out of his glorious riches he may strengthen you with power through his Spirit in your inner being, so that Christ may dwell in your hearts through faith. And I pray that you, being rooted and established in love, may have power, together with all the saints, to grasp how wide and long and high and deep is the love of Christ, and to know this love that surpasses knowledge—that you may be filled to the measure of all the fullness of God.
>
> Now to him who is able to do immeasurably more than all we ask or imagine, according to his power that is at

work within us, to him be glory in the church and in Christ Jesus throughout all generations, for ever and ever! Amen.

I often begin my teaching year by reading this prayer with my students, adding, "This is my prayer for you and me as we journey together with the Lord this term."

A second biblical passage that is deeply instructive for faith formation is Deuteronomy 6:4-9:

> Hear, O Israel: The LORD our God, the LORD is one. Love the LORD your God with all your heart and with all your soul and with all your strength. These commandments that I give you today are to be upon your hearts. Impress them on your children. Talk about them when you sit at home and when you walk along the road, when you lie down and when you get up. Tie them as symbols on your hands and bind them on your foreheads. Write them on the doorframes of your houses and on your gates.

In some orthodox Jewish homes today people still nail a tiny summary of the law onto a doorframe, and a decade ago many young people wore WWJD bracelets ("What would Jesus do?") as a reminder to follow Jesus. But the implications of the Deuteronomy passage for faith formation are not limited to literal obedience.

Four of the nine dimensions of faith formation described in these two passages above relate to the *character* of faith formation (Part 1), and the other five specifically guide us in the *activity* of faith formation (Part 2). We're inclined to rush to specific instructions for doing things, but doing that is not rooted in the bigger picture of faith formation. It's like a batter in baseball who swings as hard as he can at every pitch and becomes skilled at hitting those mile-high pop-ups. They do look impressive, but they don't accomplish anything. You will notice that this chapter links these two passages to numerous other Scripture references; groups that use this chapter for Bible study may wish to spend time lingering over some of these passages.

Part 1: The Character of Faith Formation

Faith Formation Is Christ Dwelling Within

When we peel back the layers of faith formation one by one, at the central core we find this profound mystery: Christ comes to dwell in our hearts through faith. This reality describes the Christian life after Pentecost. The Old Testament looks ahead to this mystery (Jer. 31:31-34; Joel 2:28-29), and the New Testament describes it numerous times (John 14:16-21; 17:20-23; Gal. 2:20; 4:19; Col. 1:25-27; 3:16). The Scriptures also use evocative metaphors to help us understand this mystery: Jesus is the Vine and we are branches grafted into him (John 15:1-8); we are a temple or a house that he inhabits (1 Cor. 3:9-17; 6:19-20; 1 Pet. 2:5); we are a field in which his seed has been planted (1 Cor. 3:6-9; 1 Pet. 1:18-25); we are the body of which he is the head (1 Cor. 12; Eph. 4:15-16). At the very center of our walk with God, we find the wondrous and incomprehensible mystery that the risen Lord Jesus Christ, before whom every knee shall bow, comes to live in our hearts.

What are the implications of this "indwelling" for faith formation? We need to note two. First, Christ grows within as we die to the old self and come to life in the new self. This pattern of dying and rising is a pattern of *making room*. Scripture's clearest description of this can be found in Colossians 3:1-17. After asserting our identities as new creations in Christ (vv. 1-4), Paul continues, "Put to death, therefore, whatever belongs to your earthly nature: sexual immorality, impurity, lust, evil desires and greed, which is idolatry. . . . Do not lie to each other, since you have taken off your old self with its practices and have put on the new self, which is being renewed in knowledge in the image of its Creator" (vv. 6, 9, 10). Paul then summarizes this space-making pattern, declaring, "Let the message of Christ dwell among you richly as you teach and admonish one another with all wisdom through psalms, hymns and songs from the Spirit, singing to God with gratitude in your hearts. And whatever you do, whether in word or deed, do it all in the name of the Lord Jesus, giving thanks to God the Father through him" (vv. 16-17).

Here's an illustration of how this pattern works. We live in a culture of incessant noise and activity. Almost everyone I know is too busy and too tired. This busyness and exhaustion must be put to death if Christ is to "dwell in us richly." I love to teach groups of all ages how to be still in God's presence, to ponder/pray one verse in silence for several minutes, to write reflectively about God's leading during the day, to make room for Christ to dwell within. Faith formation requires us to look inside and ask, "What is called to die in order to make more room for Christ to enter in?"

A second implication is this: we are dealing with a reality that is out of our control and beyond our understanding. Our starting point is one of humble adoration. We are servants of this "indwelling," making space for a miracle that we cannot manipulate and for which there is no technique that guarantees success.

I once spent a year walking alongside a young man who described himself as an "angry atheist." He loved to talk about the Christian faith, and the two of us had many lengthy and deep discussions. One evening he surrendered his life to the Lord during a conversation with a young woman he'd never met before who simply listened to him and wept with him. I wept with joy when I heard the news, but I knew I could never have predicted or manipulated this outcome. Thank God that the foundation of faith formation is beyond our control!

Faith Formation Is Goal-Oriented

A second characteristic of faith formation in Paul's prayer for the Ephesians points to a paradox: faith formation never ends in this life, but even so, it is goal-oriented. Paul describes the goal this way: "that you may be filled to the measure of all the fullness of God" (Eph. 3:19). Because we do not experience "arriving at the goal" in this life, it's difficult for us to imagine what that might look like. Listen to other Scriptures concerning this goal-orientation: "In all my prayers for all of you, I always pray with joy because of your partnership in the gospel from the first day until now, being confident of this, that he who began a good work in you will carry it on to completion until the day of Christ Jesus" (Phil. 1:4-6). "Dear friends, now we are children of God, and what we will be has not yet been made known. But we know that when Christ appears, we shall be like him, for we shall see him as he is" (1 John 3:2).

An anonymous preacher once said that we are "fossils of the future." Just as a fossil embedded in a rock contains the dim outline of a living organism that existed many years ago, as Christ grows in us, the dim outlines of where we are headed become apparent. All of our faith formation activity is geared toward strengthening those outlines so that the world can glimpse "new creation signposts" in our lives and communities. Singer T-Bone Burnett once put it this way:

> Sometimes I want to stop and crawl back into the womb
> And sometimes I cannot tell wrong from right
> But I ain't gonna quit until I'm laid in my tomb
> And even then they better shut it tight.
> —from "Shut It Tight"

This goal orientation has one implication for everyone who's involved in faith formation: we are to be incredibly patient and hopeful. Jesus walked the seven miles to Emmaus and then joined the two disciples for dinner before they were able to recognize him (Luke 24). God walked with Abraham and Sarah through many ups and downs until Abraham learned to trust God and obeyed the command to sacrifice his son Isaac (Gen. 12-22). Each of our faith journeys is a "jagged line" of ups and downs, but just as God patiently walks with us towards maturity in Christ, we patiently and hopefully walk with others, keeping our eyes fixed on the goal.

We Are Formed into "The People of the Story of God's Faithfulness"

The Ephesians and Deuteronomy passages quoted earlier in this chapter are two tiny excerpts from the grand story of God's faithfulness, and understanding them well requires seeing how they fit into the entire story. Moses continues the Deuteronomy passage by saying, "When the LORD your God brings you into the land he swore to your fathers, to Abraham, Isaac and Jacob, to give you—a land with large, flourishing cities you did not build, houses filled with all kinds of good things you did not provide, wells you did not dig, and vineyards and olive groves you did not plant—then when you eat and are satisfied, be careful that you do not forget the Lord, who brought you out of Egypt, out of the land of slavery" (vv. 10-12). In other words, the commandments you are called to obey are not just random laws dictated by an arbitrary King; these commandments form you into the people who live inside the story of God's faithfulness.

The freed Israelites continually complained and wanted to go back to Egypt. They considered the story of Egypt's food supplies more attractive than the story of God's liberating faithfulness (Num. 11; 20:1-5), and their character and lifestyles fit more with the story of Egypt than with the story of God. As one commentator pointed out, after God took his people out of Egypt, God faced the more challenging task of taking Egypt out of his people.

When television first became popular in the 1950s, commercials were thirty-second logical arguments for buying a particular product. Those commercials were not all that effective. Then marketers discovered that a thirty-second short story featuring the product in the lives of its characters was much more powerful. They discovered a biblical truth: people are shaped by stories. And that is why the Scriptures contain hundreds of stories. Woven together, all those stories tell the one great story of God creating and redeeming the world.

Faith formation always occurs at the intersection between two stories: the story of God and the story of our culture. If we do not identify both stories, the story of our culture will hinder and choke our growth as a people shaped by the story of God's faithfulness, just as thorns choked the sower's seed (Mark 4:7, 18-19). Faith formation intentionally shapes us inside the story of God and exposes the falsehood of the stories of our culture.

Faith Formation Is Bathed in Prayer

Paul's words in the Ephesians 3 passage are not so much a *teaching about* faith formation as a *prayer for* faith formation. Imagine a stage with a large circle of light coming from an overhead spotlight. All of our faith formation activities take place inside the circle of God's presence within that spotlight. Whatever we do there, we surrender to God's leading and working in ways that are far richer than we can ever know. So every time we drive home from another class or end another activity, a voice in our hearts declares with Paul, "Now to him who is able to do immeasurably more than all we ask or imagine, according to his power that is at work within us, to him be glory in the church and in Christ Jesus throughout all generations, for ever and ever! Amen" (Eph. 3:20-21).

Part 2: The Activity of Faith Formation

From the Lord's perspective, faith formation is not first of all a program but a 24/7 life walk: God is forming us all the time, and the activity of faith formation is always happening. Therefore, our efforts to understand this activity always have a dual dimension: we're trying to understand something the Lord is always doing, and we want to replicate its dimensions in our specific programming. With that in mind, we'll explore these five dimensions.

Faith Formation Takes Place "Together with All the Saints"

Take a moment to name four people who have played a significant role in your own faith formation. Recall the various ways in which they've blessed you: their character, lifestyle, piety, words of encouragement and challenge, the ways they loved you through both good and hard times. The Lord's poignant observation concerning Adam—"It is not good for the man to be alone" (Gen. 2:18)—also applies to faith formation. *We need each other* to grow in our faith. Just as the Hebrews were told to remember the mighty cloud of witnesses who encouraged them to fix their eyes on Jesus and run the race set before them (Heb. 12:1-2), so God calls us to name our mighty cloud and know that we are part of the cloud that blesses many others.

Paul reminds us that faith formation takes place together with *all* the saints. So I encourage youth pastors to form leadership teams that include at least one grandparent. Recently friends of ours had a newborn baby with Down syndrome. After listening to their coming to terms with this and praying with them, our pastor told them, "I know that your child will bring tremendous blessings to our congregation." He recognized that our walk with God is deepened and enriched when a wide variety of God's children walk together.

Picture the past year of faith formation in your own life and in the lives of those closest to you. Have there been regular opportunities for meaningful interaction between people of various ages and life experiences? Do you get to hear the testimonies of God's goodness and the realities of human struggle in your worship? Are guests invited to tell their stories? Does your church bring people together for service projects who may not "naturally" work side by side? How have you experienced faith formation "together with all the saints," and how might this togetherness be enhanced?

Moses' teaching in Deuteronomy adds another dimension to this theme: faith formation involves "all the saints," but the family plays a special role. The church is called to *supplement and support* faith nurture in the home, but because many homes are harried and stressed, the church often *replaces* the calling of the home instead. One of the tasks of churches (and Christian schools) is to ask, "How can we partner with parents in faith nurture activities? What challenges do they face, and what can we provide to encourage them to work through these challenges?"

Faith Formation Involves Lifelong Maturation

Whenever I try to picture Paul's challenge to grasp "how wide and long and high and deep is the love of Christ," I imagine a three-dimensional shape that stretches above the clouds, into the depths of the oceans, and beyond the horizon in all directions. In this life, we never fully comprehend the vastness of Christ's love for us, and therefore faith formation never ends. As an elderly apostle in prison, Paul makes the same point in a very different way:

> I want to know Christ—yes, to know the power of his resurrection and participation in his sufferings, becoming

like him in his death, and so, somehow, attaining to the resurrection from the dead.

Not that I have already obtained all this, or have already arrived at my goal, but I press on to take hold of that for which Christ Jesus took hold of me. Brothers and sisters, I do not consider myself yet to have taken hold of it. But one thing I do: Forgetting what is behind and straining toward what is ahead, I press on toward the goal to win the prize for which God has called me heavenward in Christ Jesus (Phil. 3:10-14).

It must have been very encouraging for the believers in Philippi to hear their chief teacher and mentor describe his own need to continue maturing in Christ, even as he dared to say to them, "Whatever you have learned or received or heard from me, or seen in me—put it into practice" (Phil. 4:9).

When churches, homes, or schools tacitly communicate that children and teens are in the midst of faith formation but that the adults have "arrived," everyone's faith formation suffers. But that's what happens when we gear almost all the faith formation programming to those under twenty-five, when we identify the younger ones as the ones with questions and the older folks as the ones with answers, when we rarely acknowledge the struggles and confusion of adults over twenty-five. I'll never forget the teen who said, "One of the teachers who helped me the most was quick to say, 'I don't know' when I asked him a difficult question about the Christian faith. He'd say, 'I've struggled with that question too, and this is where my struggling has taken me, but I can't give you a neat and tidy answer.' He was like an older brother walking alongside me, and that was very encouraging."

Picture the faith formation activities and assumptions in your community and ask yourself, "What tacit messages does this picture send to our community about lifelong faith formation?"

Faith Formation Is Paradoxical: Knowing Love That Surpasses Knowledge

Our three children came into our family through adoption. Our youngest spent the first seven months of his life with a foster family; during the adoption process we spent quite a bit of time with that family. About a month after he moved into our home, my wife and I sent the family a card that said, "Thank you for loving him so that he knows what it means to be loved. The gift you gave him has blessed him tremendously as he is adjusting to our home and family."

Faith formation involves "knowing love that surpasses knowledge." In discussions about faith formation, people are apt to say something like this: "Too often church education programs tell us a great deal about God without bringing us into relationship with him." In other words, faith *information* adds to our pool of knowledge about God; faith *formation* reshapes our heart to receive God's love more fully. Jesus makes a similar distinction when he says to the Pharisees, "You study the Scriptures diligently because you think that in them you possess eternal life. These are the very Scriptures that testify about me, yet you refuse to come to me to have life" (John 5:39-40). They wanted knowledge without relationship. More accurately, they used their knowledge to stifle relationship.

Because this formation/information contrast is so prevalent in church education today, some people assume that information about God is at best irrelevant and at worst is actually a hindrance to growing a deeper relationship with him. But that assumption has no biblical basis whatsoever. We have received the story of God's faithfulness to us woven through the Bible's 1,189 chapters—chapters that demand high levels of biblical literacy and careful study. If this story is to form us, surely we are called to digest and appropriate a great deal of information. Why else would so much of the Bible's teaching be focused on correcting misinformation? Information about God is not the center of faith formation, but it is indispensable in coming to know how wide and long and high and deep is the love of God.

Before our three children joined our family, my wife, Evelyn, and I sought to learn as much as we could about their lives. This information became a support that strengthened our love for each child. Similarly, faith formation is focused on knowing and receiving God's love; knowing the shape of God's heart and the many ways he has been faithful supports our experience of that love. What faith formation activities have helped you to strengthen your love of God? What do activities that strengthen love look like?

Faith Formation Requires Spiritual Disciplines

We walk in God's presence every moment of our lives (Ps. 139). Although God is always at work forming us, we are often blind to his formative presence. And in our blindness we live on a spiritual "autopilot." In this passage it's as if Moses is saying, "Wake up! Surround yourselves with reminders of God's character and faithfulness. Remember that you're called to live in a way that's consistent with who God is." Today we call these regular wake-up calls "spiritual disciplines." We engage in these activities to declare, "I want to become more like Christ."

Participating in worship and attending church education classes are spiritual disciplines, as are daily prayer and Scripture reading, practicing generosity and hospitality, promoting justice, accepting people on the margins of society, receiving God's gifts with thanksgiving, fasting—the list could go on and on. All these are part of a larger fabric of spiritual disciplines, the fabric of "hands and foreheads, doorframes and gates" that combine to carry out the Lord's formative work.

In our churches, homes, and schools we need to ask, "What does the larger fabric look like? Where are the weak spots in the whole picture that need shoring up? What is my particular involvement within the whole picture?" A church education teacher once said to me, "Years ago my teaching was sequential; I could build on themes from week to week. Now only about half the students come each week, a different group each time. So my teaching has to be episodic: each lesson needs to stand completely on its own and can't build on previous ones. That makes teaching much more difficult."

She identified a weak spot in the fabric of spiritual disciplines, one you may be able to identify with. Perhaps many of our communities need to be (re)educated concerning the need for hands, foreheads, doorframes, and gates in our lives.

Faith Formation Requires Biblical Literacy

The divine revelation Moses' audience received as he spoke the words of Deuteronomy 6 to them can be summarized as "these commandments" (v. 6), and Moses instructed the people to become thoroughly acquainted with them. Today we have the entire Old and New Testament Scriptures, and that requirement still stands. We need to be thoroughly acquainted with them. That's a daunting challenge! But our knowledge of the Scriptures grows as we gradually work at it year by year; we have a lifetime to mature toward biblical literacy.

Does it really matter in this electronic age when you can enter a word or phrase into a search engine like biblegateway.com and find whatever you need instantly? Computer programs are wonderful tools, but they can never replace the need for biblical literacy. As the Word lives in our hearts, it shapes our character, our speech, our prayers, our perceptions.

Here's an illustration of why biblical literacy matters. Many Christians are deeply moved by David's simple declaration of trust in Psalm 23: "The Lord is my shepherd." The biblically literate believer weaves this declaration into her heart. She knows that Jesus is the good shepherd who has lain down his life for his sheep (John 10:11), and that his shepherding work took place within the profound paradox of becoming a Lamb (John 1:29; Rev. 7:17). She understands that this paradox points to the deep truth that in Christ God's power is made perfect in weakness (2 Cor. 12:9). And she takes to heart the reminder to feed his lambs and take care of his sheep (John 21:15-17). Biblical literacy makes room for what we might call 1 + 1 = 3 math: as we combine various Scriptures together, a much richer and fuller picture emerges, and we are able to discern our own place in God's story.

Because these nine biblical characteristics of faith formation are all interrelated, it is easy to summarize them in one paragraph: Our faith is formed during a lifetime of maturing in Christ. We experience his love more and more as we become more like him. Christ lives in us through his Spirit, and because we have been grafted into his body, our faith is formed together with all the saints. On the one hand, this process is a profound mystery that we surrender to God in prayer; on the other, it includes practicing a web of spiritual disciplines to make room for Christ to dwell in us. As we do so, the old self dies and the new self comes to life. This includes putting to death the false stories of our culture so that we can be shaped by the true story of God's faithfulness. The better acquainted we are with God's story, the more available we are to be transformed by it. Our love for God and our experience of God's love is deepened and strengthened when we share our knowledge about him.

Like you, I will be involved in leading specific faith formation activities this year. The picture that helps me hold these nine dimensions together is the description of Jesus walking with two discouraged disciples to Emmaus in Luke 24. He lovingly enters into their lostness, patiently walks alongside them, and immerses them in the biblical story. Finally he breaks bread with them and they recognize him. The fact that Jesus' seven-mile-long sermon was not enough to restore their faith reminds me what a mystery faith formation is! The fact that Jesus stayed with them until they recognized him reminds me to persevere, to continue sowing seeds I do not control. And when an insecure voice inside me wants quicker, more predictable results, I add these words to the Emmaus picture: "Sow your seed in the morning, and at evening let your hands not be idle, for you do not know which will succeed, whether this or that, or whether both will do equally well" (Eccl. 11: 6). Those words encourage me once again to take up the profound privilege of walking with others to Emmaus.

Chapter 2

Embodied Wisdom:
Faith Formation through Faith Practices

Don C. Richter

Christian *practices are not activities we do to make something spiritual happen in our lives. Nor are they duties we undertake to be obedient to God. Rather, they are patterns of communal action that create openings in our lives where the grace, mercy, and presence of God may be made known to us. They are places where the power of God is experienced. In the end, these are not ultimately our practices but forms of participation in the practice of God.*[1]

Where Faith Begins

For almost everyone, faith begins in practice rather than belief.[2] At bedtime a young child chants "Now I lay me down to sleep, I pray the Lord my soul to keep." At the dinner table another child sings the Johnny Appleseed blessing: "Oh, the Lord is good to me, and so I thank the Lord." On a mission trip, a youth group reads the Bible and helps a local congregation repair homes. A middle-aged man bakes a loaf of bread for a fellow choir member who has just had surgery. An eighty-year-old woman grooms her hair and trims and polishes her nails every Saturday evening. She carefully considers which dress to wear to Sunday school and worship.

Where does faith begin? Faith begins in practice, in words and songs and gestures and things we do with and for our bodies, with and for one another. We learn to pray by praying. We learn to serve by serving. We learn to care by concrete acts of caring—not by vague expressions of goodwill. Sometimes the words are explicitly religious (*Lord, pray*), sometimes implicitly so (*bread, clothing*). Informed by the stories and imagery of Christian faith, each of the above activities is charged with meaning and purpose.

Throughout her life, the elderly woman has "honored the Lord's day" by bathing and wearing special clothes. As a young child, she delighted in dressing up and attending church with her family; as a youth, she sometimes resented doing so. Still she persisted in this practice, year after year, when her heart was in it and when it was not. Such a quaint habit, dressing up for church. . . .

At age eighty, the woman has outlived both parents. She thinks of them with affection and gratitude as she lays out her Sunday outfit. As a breast cancer survivor, the woman has felt shame and sadness about her aging body. Grooming her hair and nails restores her dignity and fills her with healthy pride in her appearance. She also enjoys the company. Every Saturday evening, a younger woman from her church joins her for dinner, conversation, and a manicure.

Such a quaint habit, dressing up for church . . . and yet, after a lifetime, this activity is charged with meaning and purpose. It may take a lifetime to appreciate the significance of such an activity, to grasp its many levels of meaning, to receive it as a means of grace.

Or perhaps dressing up for church can take on deeper meaning even now, even for young people. Teens serving in mission read Scripture about clothing themselves with Christ (Gal. 3:27) as they put on work clothes each day to serve others. Dusty and sweaty after hours of hard labor, they're eager to clean up and dress for an evening praise service. Returning home, they're thankful for abundant hot water whenever they bathe. For a while—a few weeks, perhaps—these young people gladly dress up for worship. For years to come, some of them will wear simple crosses fashioned from nails—a gift from their mission partner congregation. As they dress for church, they will put these crosses around their necks and think of their distant brothers and sisters in Christ with special affection and gratitude.

Playing and Praying

Faith begins in practice, at whatever age one comes to faith—child, teen, or adult.[3] We begin with simple skills and move toward the more complex. It's like learning to play the piano. No one is born knowing how to play the instrument. Even those with aptitude or strong musical intelligence[4] must first learn the basics. Beginners—age five or fifty—learn to read music and practice scales. Advanced players still rehearse the basics over and over. The best pianists in the world are not merely "naturals," but have spent thousands of hours honing their keyboard skills.[5]

No one is born knowing how to pray. Though everyone may be endowed with a "restless heart," as Augustine called it, that seeks communion with God, prayer is a practice that must be learned *from* and *with* others. At age five or fifty, we begin with the basics: prayer posture, simple prayers for bedtime and meals, Psalm 23, the Lord's Prayer. Learning prayers "by heart," we internalize the logic, structure, and language of prayer.[6] We learn fitting ways to pray in different circumstances, and how to lead others in prayer.

Every practice involves particular kinds of knowledge and ways of knowing. As an artistic practice, playing the piano encompasses a vast repertoire of music theory and performance skills. But not every practitioner has to master this whole range of information. The beginner can play a simple piece by Mozart without understanding all the compositional elements or the history of Mozart interpretation. In time, learning such knowledge may deepen and enhance individual performance—as long as the pianist continues practicing basic scales! Because this is communal activity, shared by practitioners over time, plunking notes on the keyboard (kinesthetic knowing) is integrally linked to the conceptual, "grammatical" understanding of music as harmony, rhythm, melody, and the like. Practitioners at every level are linked by common practice.

Faith practices too involve particular kinds of knowledge and ways of knowing. We generally absorb the know-how we need in the course of practicing over time. As with playing the piano or speaking a language, the "grammar" rules often remain implicit in early stages of learning. When Jesus' disciples asked him, "Lord, teach us to pray, just as John taught his disciples" (Luke 11:1), Jesus didn't lecture them on the history of petitionary prayer. He taught them a simple prayer, the Lord's Prayer.

Embedded in Jesus' simple prayer are grammar rules that have shaped Christian prayer across the centuries. These grammar rules, or doctrines, don't float down from on high. They emerge from the very down-to-earth practices Jesus taught his followers. They are not set in stone, but continue to be interpreted and modified as faith practices are adapted to different times and places. Christian doctrines are a conceptual way of knowing within a faith practice, much as music theory is a conceptual way of knowing the piano.

Practice-Shaped Beliefs

Miroslav Volf, a systematic theologian, teaches and writes about the conceptual beliefs that undergird Christian faith. Volf observes that sometimes people engage in Christian practices because they find Christian beliefs intellectually compelling. As a rule, he notes, this is not how things happen:

> People come to believe either because they find themselves already engaged in Christian practices (say, by being raised in a Christian home) or because they are attracted to them. In most cases, Christian practices come first and Christian beliefs follow—or rather, beliefs are already entailed in practices, so that their explicit espousing becomes a matter of bringing to consciousness what is implicit in the engagement of the practices themselves.[7]

Volf recounts how he himself grew in faith through his parents' practice of Christian hospitality.[8] Volf was raised in Yugoslavia, where his father pastored a small Pentecostal congregation. Once a month, a guest from the back country would join his family for worship and Sunday dinner. Young Volf was disgusted by the way this "rough-hewn and slightly menacing figure" would loudly slurp his soup at every meal. He resented his parents for repeatedly inviting this ill-mannered stranger to their house, thereby ruining his favorite meal.

In hindsight, Volf realizes how profoundly his parents grasped the integrity of Christian belief and practice. Welcoming this stranger to the Lord's Table meant also welcoming him to their household table. Had he protested, his parents would have reminded him that when the Great Banquet is served at the end of time, he must be prepared to sit next to this very man he despised. Belief shaped practice; practice reinforced belief. And by participating in this practice over time, even when his heart was not in it, Volf came to appreciate, accept, and eventually articulate the beliefs that informed this practice.

> People make Christian beliefs their own and understand them in particular ways partly because of the practices to which they have been introduced—in which their souls and bodies have been trained—in the course of their lives.[9]

Several points are worth noting about the relationship between Christian beliefs and practices. First, *practice-shaped beliefs are resilient.* Volf acknowledges his parents as exemplary practitioners of hospitality. Yet as a young man he rejected faith precisely because his parents' ardent practices had such a strong claim upon his life. Later, reclaimed by faith, Volf realized how those practice-shaped beliefs knit in his bones persisted in their influence, even during a period of doubt. Good seed continued to germinate, despite drought and neglect.

Second, *practice-shaped beliefs hold practitioners accountable.* Volf claims that even if his parents had been hypocritical practitioners of hospitality, the church's Great Tradition still could have inscribed gospel-oriented belief on his heart. Even if his parents had refused to invite back their guest after his initial visit, the liturgy of the Lord's Supper might have apprenticed young Volf in gracious table fellowship practices. As youth often do, he might then have challenged his parents, "Practice what you preach!" And he might have made a determined effort to become a more welcoming host himself.

Third, *practice-shaped beliefs must be strengthened by wider communities of practice.* Christian practices are not pure, ideal forms; crystal goblets fated to shatter whenever they're filled with real people and institutions. The practices are blemished and imperfect vessels, already cracked and broken, yet bearers of God's grace. "But we have this treasure in jars of clay," Paul says, "to show that this all-surpassing power is from God and not from us" (2 Cor. 4:7). At every level—family, congregation, judicatory, global church— households of faith mutually support and correct one another in strengthening faithful practice.[10]

Finally, Christians come to understand that *practice-shaped beliefs* *also shape our practices*. Beliefs shape performance, give grammar a framework, and present a worldview that makes sense of our practices. Beliefs hold practices accountable and evaluate their integrity. Christian formation includes learning beliefs and discussing them as part of our life together in community. Respecting the faith-shaping power of beliefs, the Reformers crafted catechisms to promote such conversation, to provide scaffolding for faith, and to enable disciples to "talk themselves into being Christian."[11]

Joining God's Practice

The ancient Hebrews understood faith as way of life to be shaped in every domain: "when you sit at home and when walk along the road, when you lie down and when you get up" (Deut. 6:7). They did not consider faith practices to be "spiritual" or "religious" activities separate from daily life. A practice such as keeping Sabbath, which seems explicitly religious, actually has much broader implications. Beginning with the Ten Commandments, Sabbath observance was commended for the welfare of all—not only the Hebrews themselves but foreigners, animals, and even the land itself. Observing a day of rest each week is vital to human flourishing, regardless of a person's faith convictions.[12] Jesus reminded the Pharisees of this when he told them, "The Sabbath was made for people, not people for the Sabbath" (Mark 2:27).

The bold claim of Sabbath observance is that this practice draws us into God's intentions for us and for the world. It may sound presumptuous to suggest that creatures participate in the Creator's activity, but the Hebrew Scriptures invite us to embrace that presumption, contesting the view that "God is watching us from a distance," impassively musing about human misfortune while remaining above the fray. These Scriptures bear witness to an evolving, covenantal relationship between Creator and creatures.

Christians confess that God's covenant with creation became embodied in Jesus of Nazareth. Taking on an earthly body, God waded into the flow of history to offer welcome and share table fellowship, to forgive sins and heal bodies. In Christ, all humankind has been invited to participate in these life-giving practices. The question Christians need to ask is not, "What would Jesus do?"—speculating about how the historical Jesus might react to a given situation. Rather, the pivotal question is, "How can we join Jesus in his life-giving ministry in and for the sake of the world?"

Jesus' first followers asked themselves this question. They shared food, shelter, fellowship, music, clothing, money, and caretaking responsibilities—not only with family and friends, but also with neighbors, strangers, and even oppressors.[13] From the outset, the community gathered around Jesus proclaimed that faith is not an add-on to life but the fertile ground that enables life to flourish. For every creaturely need and condition, the life of faith provides wise pathways and grace-full patterns of behaving and believing. We call these pathways and patterns *Christian practices*.

Embodied Wisdom

Christian practices are things Christians do attentively . . . together . . . in the real world . . . for the sake of all . . . in response to God.[14] Offering welcome, managing our stuff, keeping Sabbath, forgiving—these are basic *human practices*, essential to the well-being of individuals and the welfare of every society. People the world over already participate in these practices to some extent, whether informed by faith or not. Christian faith infuses these practices with particular substance, power, and depth. Christian faith baptizes these activity clusters, and God uses them as *means of grace* to nourish and sustain the life of faith in particular settings.

A "practices" approach to faith formation notices the way of life that emerges among Christians—right here among us today, and across cultures and millennia—as people live in response to God's grace. The educational task is to notice, name, and nurture practice connections with Scripture and worship and the world, so that our way of life will be more life-giving for us and others.

Christian practices offer embodied wisdom in a world that values *choice*. Our consumer-based economy celebrates the human capacity to choose a product or service from a menu of available options. But what enables us to choose wisely and well? How do we discover a promising path that may not be featured on the latest map? How do we discern a wise course of action that may not be apparent from consulting only the most up-to-date sources?

Disciples don't have to start from scratch in every successive generation. Historical figures as well as people within our own community become wise and trusted companions for the journey. Their wisdom is not like perfume—an essence distilled in a bottle and doled out in fragrant drops at whim. Nor is wisdom a proverbial strand of pearls that one person can simply hand over to another.[15] Instead, we immerse ourselves in a community of skilled practitioners, trusting that over time, wisdom will be knit into our bones as our life together becomes more attuned to the challenging claims of the gospel.

Wisdom is not static. Being wise means knowing how to size up a situation, discerning what to keep and what needs to be changed. A wise cook knows when to follow a recipe closely and when to adapt. The lack of ingredients—or access to new ones—may lead to new culinary creations. And in a stage production, a wise actor knows how to improvise when a prop doesn't work or a fellow actor forgets a line. So it is with Christian practices, which must be reimagined and adapted afresh in every new context and era. The more we rehearse and perform, the better equipped we become to improvise when the unexpected happens—which it eventually will.

Practicing in Context

As we have seen, Christian practices are not reducible to "congregational practices." Yet the local congregation can be a hub for intentional formation in faith practices, especially as parish programs are transfigured by grace. A congregation's practice of hospitality, for example, may begin with good signage, designated greeters, and visitor nametags. Blessed and broken, these basic welcoming gestures can lead to deeper awareness of and participation in God's gracious hospitality. Consider the following examples.

- In the center of a university town, a historic church spends a season pondering how to deepen its practice of hospitality.

Members of the congregation study and pray together over meals in each others' homes. They share personal stories of welcoming and being welcomed by others. Instead of dismissing the children midway through the worship service, leaders equip young people as liturgists. During one communion service, children gather at the Lord's Table to make sandwiches. Following the service, they take their offering outside to feed hungry people on the city streets.

- A small rural church studies the history of Christian hospitality over the course of a year.[16] Opening themselves "to the joy and surprise that we encounter in the hospitality of Jesus," they expand the capacity of the community food pantry to assist many neighbors affected by hard times. They also design a "hospitality directory" for welcoming new and prospective members into service and fellowship. According to their pastor, this directory signifies a decisive shift in outlook "from survival to service." Community members rally in support of the church's hospitality ministry, contributing food from local farms and businesses, "like the multiplication of loaves and fishes."

In both cases, disciples desired to be more faithful in practicing Christian hospitality. They didn't have a game plan for where this would lead. Their discernment process was not always encouraging and good-natured. They fumbled at times, waiting for wisdom to illumine their next steps. Yet they trusted Christ to bless, break, and use their blemished and imperfect efforts, transforming them into a means of grace for themselves and for others.

In addition to the local congregation, and especially for young people, the home remains a primary context for forming faith through the daily tasks of living together as a household.[17] Recall the lessons Miroslav Volf learned about Christian hospitality from his parents. Other potential settings for cultivating Christian practices include

- a residential camp and conference center in which people share life together over a period of time;[18]

- an intentional Christian community in which young adults share a household and try to be mindful about the practices that shape their shared way of life, including economic practices, Sabbath-keeping, hospitality, and prayer;[19]

- a community choir in which people of diverse backgrounds gather to sing their lives to God, and occasionally to break bread;[20]

- an outreach ministry that provides clean water and hygiene education to communities in need.[21]

Learning Over a Lifetime

To be human is to grow and develop. A practices approach to formation is concerned with how such growth and development occur *in faith*. The emphasis shifts from the developmental capacities of individuals to the development of Christian practices within communities. With teenagers, for example, the framework becomes "growing in faith with youth" instead of "youth ministry" being something adults do to or for young people. While Christian practices are by nature multigenerational, significant learning can take place within age groups and life stage groups as well.

Learning practices can involve us in confronting big ethical dilemmas, figuring out small ways to make others feel more welcome, and everything in between. One "practice move" to notice and name—and a good place to begin—involves the many ways one can be faithful by *not* doing something: *not* littering helps care for the earth; *not* checking email on Sunday invites Sabbath keeping; *not* impulse buying promotes good stewardship. Like decluttering a room, it's liberating to realize that *not* taking on one more task can open the door to grace.

Often a practice is taught implicitly, under the radar, as when a congregation uses Fair Trade coffee for all church functions as a gesture of solidarity with coffee growers from distant lands. Parishioners may buy and use Fair Trade coffee at home, out of habit, without pausing to ponder the implications of their actions. Other times teaching a practice is direct and explicit. When an inner-city church trains members to serve in their "Breaking Bread" ministry with homeless neighbors, clear and concise instructions are given for how to prepare meals, engage guests, and deal with disruptive behavior. Prayer, Bible study, and reading about homelessness and the ethics of Christian hospitality also foster learning among those who serve.[22]

It is the challenge and privilege of Christians to live the abundant life of Christian practices not in the abstract, but in concrete, particular places: in their own family, neighborhood, school, or town. Quite often we discover the growing edge of our faith as we practice it in our own backyards.

In a small Midwestern city, parishioners noticed that the residents of a nearby apartment building regularly cut through the church property, resulting in an unsightly dirt pathway. Instead of fortifying the fence, the church improved and lighted the path and planted vegetable and herb gardens nearby. Church members invited neighbors to help grow and cultivate the vegetables, building new relationships among people and with the soil. The challenge of a "trespass" became an opportunity to practice caring for the earth alongside neighbors in need.

Embracing the challenge does not mean viewing practices as a new legalism or form of works righteousness. Dorothy Bass notes,

> There is something in our human nature that looks at a list of good things and sees only a catalogue of demands. You should! You must! Follow the rules! Multiple "oughts" weigh in so heavily on us that we forget to notice and lean on the freeing power of the Holy Spirit. To see the world and God through the thick lenses of obligation does not lead to a way of life abundant.[23]

Practices are a gift before they are a task. They are channels of grace for us and for those we serve, not ways of showing God, ourselves, or other people how good we are. "The Christian faith is not primarily about human doing but about human receiving," Volf reminds us. "The barebones formal injunction to which the gospel can be reduced is, 'Receive yourself and your world as a new creation.'"[24]

Worship is both the source and summit of Christian discipleship. Through our worship, we are ritually formed in all Christian practices, strengthened in learning them over a lifetime, and sent forth into the world to practice them with others. Gathered in worship, we both offer and receive ourselves and our world as a new creation. Worship reminds us that the chief end of humankind, as Calvin claimed, is "to glorify God and enjoy God forever." As we turn to God and rehearse our destiny, worship creates "openings in our lives where the grace, mercy, and presence of God may be made known to us." In and through worship, we are humbled by the realization that Christian practices "are not ultimately our practices but forms of participation in the practice of God."[25]

Chapter 3

Distinguishing Dragons:

The Importance of Story in Faith Formation

Sarah Arthur

"There was a boy," wrote C. S. Lewis, "called Eustace Clarence Scrubb, and he almost deserved it." So begins one of the most beloved children's stories of all time, *The Voyage of the Dawn Treader*.[1] Lewis goes on to describe this boy as a spoiled brat with no imagination. Eustace knows nothing of stories, tales of high adventure, or heroes with virtuous codes of honor. The only books Eustace likes are "books of information." This is a problem. Not only is Eustace about to go on a very great adventure—sailing with the King of Narnia to the edge of the world—but his imagination is so stunted that he is singularly ill-equipped to act in meaningful ways when faced with critical decisions.

Take dragons, for instance. When Eustace sees one, alone on a deserted island, he has no idea what he is looking at. That's because Eustace has "read only the wrong books. They had a lot to say about exports and imports and governments and drains, but they were weak on dragons."[2] He has no idea that when he enters the dragon's cave, he had better not fall asleep on the pile of sharp objects littering the floor because if you fall asleep on a dragon's hoard, you become a dragon yourself. Only after he becomes a dragon does he begin to understand how ill-prepared he is for this adventure. One of his shipmates—his old enemy, the valiant mouse Reepicheep— takes pity on him and tries to offer encouragement. And how does the mouse do so? By telling stories. Since Eustace had read only the wrong books, Reepicheep sets out to explain that what has happened to Eustace is a pattern easily found in tales about great men "who had fallen from prosperity into the most distressing circumstances, and of whom many had recovered and lived happily ever afterwards."[3] Eventually Eustace is converted (and yes, it is a kind of baptism) back into a boy by the powerful Lion, Aslan; in time he grows into a virtuous character who's worthy of the tale in which he finds himself.

The transformation of Eustace is helpful for understanding something vital about the Christian life: *We are story-formed people.* Our lives are first shaped by narrative, not by information. We don't learn how to live the Christian life by memorizing facts, rules, precepts, morals, imports, exports, governments, and drains. Instead, from our earliest moments we experience the stories of those who have gone before us: stories from the Old and New Testaments; stories from the history of the Church throughout the centuries; stories of our own families and local congregations; stories that are enacted each week in the drama we call worship and in the everyday conversations and practices of the home. Through these stories we learn to recognize dragons when we see them. We begin to see our lives as part of a pattern within the larger story of redemption. We long to live a life worthy of that story. We begin to desire the right things. And such longing shapes our habits of thought (imagination) and our habits of action (practices) so that in time we are able to act instinctively for the good in the critical moment.

The problem is, many of us have been taught that being a Christian means, first, agreeing to a bunch of facts. God exists: that's a fact. Jesus is the Son of God: that's another fact. If we've got the facts straight, we think we've got the faith straight. The place where we get those facts is the Bible. Therefore we think the Bible is *first of all* a book of information, like the encyclopedia; it's a textbook. Is it any wonder that we read the Bible with about as much enthusiasm as we read the periodic table of the elements? In the beginning was hydrogen, helium, lithium, beryllium—and there will be a test on Tuesday.

Certainly facts are important, and the Bible contains the most important information we will ever need. Scattered throughout its pages are vital theological statements such as "the wages of sin is death" (Rom. 6:23) and "God is spirit, and those who worship him must worship in spirit and truth" (John 4:24).[4] Sermons are preached (Matt. 5-7), letters sent (1 John; Jude), and eloquent theological arguments constructed (1 Cor. 15). There are journalistic facts too, such as lists of those who died in the wilderness (in Numbers) similar to the Vietnam War Memorial. But such moments of teaching or journalistic information are few compared to the narrative dramas that surround them.

In fact, we almost could envision the Bible as someone's scrapbook. Accompanying every snapshot, every ticket stub, every snatch of musical lyrics is a person sitting next to you, narrating the events—and not necessarily in chronological order. "Oh, yeah, that was the day Moses got so angry. And here's another picture of the pillar of cloud, with Grandma Miriam singing to the right there; isn't she lovely? (That was before she got sick, of course. Poor thing.) I wrote down the song somewhere—ah, yes, here it is. . . ." None of the informative parts of Scripture make sense apart from the stories in which they are embedded, or apart from the narrative voice of the community as it tells and retells those stories.

"Who is my neighbor?" someone once asked Jesus in Luke 10:29. Our Lord did not reply with an abstract doctrine of human beings made in the image of God, "fallen from communion with God, under his wrath and curse, and so made liable to all the miseries of this life, to death itself, and to the pains of hell forever."[5] Yikes! Rather, he said, "Once there was a man going down from Jerusalem to Jericho, who fell into the hands of robbers. . . ." When Moses encountered God in the burning bush in Exodus 3, God did not introduce himself by saying that he is "a Spirit, infinite, eternal, and unchangeable, in my being, wisdom, power, holiness, justice, goodness, and truth."[6] Rather, God said, "I am the God of your father, the God of Abraham, the God of Isaac, and the God of Jacob." God located his own character within a narrative of relationship to a particular people whom Moses knew well. Even in Deuteronomy—a book as full of rules and regulations, precepts and principles, as anyone could ever wish to see—the people are told, "When your children ask you in time to come, 'What is the meaning of the decrees and the statutes and the ordinances that the Lord our God has commanded you?'" (Deut. 6:20), the answer is not abstract theological statements but storytelling: "Then you shall say to your children, 'We were Pharaoh's slaves in Egypt, but the Lord brought us out of Egypt with a mighty hand. . . .'" And they are to tell the whole tale.

It is not merely *recommended* that we tell the Bible as story; it is *commanded*.

So the Bible is not *first of all* a book of information. That is its secondary purpose. First of all, the Bible is a story. From the opening poem of Genesis to the closing hymn of Revelation, the Bible is a master narrative that takes place with particular characters, in particular settings, along particular plotlines, using particular tones or "voices" unique to its authors, and using a host of literary genres—from poetry to prose, drama to hymn, parable to prophetic word, and everything in between. In short, our text is not a textbook. It is a tale of high adventure with breathtaking, heartbreaking, bedazzling twists and turns. No wonder medieval Christians called the Good News the "good spell"—the enchanting tale that is the root of our word *gospel!*[7]

What would happen to our engagement with Scripture—at church and at home—if we thought of it as a story? How might that change the way we read, teach, and discuss the Bible? The following are some beginning thoughts on how to approach the Bible as narrative in three overlapping zones: in communal worship, through Christian education (such as Sunday school and Bible studies), and at home.

First, communal worship: The chief place where we encounter the Bible as story is not in the privacy of our bedrooms but in the communal drama of worship on a Sunday morning. Indeed, worship itself is the story of Scripture performed like a Passion play, a story whose chapters unfold throughout the seasons of the liturgical year—beginning with Advent and moving through Epiphany, Lent, Holy Week, Pentecost, and Ordinary Time. It is a story of redemption performed every time we enact the Lord's Supper: "On the night when Jesus was arrested. . . ." And it isn't just the pastor or worship leaders who do the performing while everyone else sits back and watches: it is the entire worshiping community—from the liturgist at the lectern to the people in the pews to the nannies in the nursery—who *together* tell the story of God's creating, redeeming, sustaining grace. It is a story into which we are invited, a story that began long before we got here and will continue long after we're gone. If we think of worship that way, we might be less inclined to skip a Sunday! It would be like skipping an episode of our favorite TV drama.

Meanwhile, there are moments in the service in which we open the pages of Scripture and hear a *specific* story or passage proclaimed. The liturgist or pastor reads the passage aloud and then preaches a message that considers the passage more in depth. Unfortunately, many of us have been conditioned with a little "off" switch when this happens. We switch from story-loving creatures waiting to be enchanted (the way we are when we settle in to watch a movie at the theater) to patients waiting in line for a prescription refill. We switch into the zone of boredom because we assume that whatever lies ahead will be difficult and unpleasant. Even the best liturgists may find themselves reading the assigned text as if reading aloud from the telephone book—with even less familiarity with its names and pronunciations. Yet hand the liturgist a copy of *Grimm's Fairy Tales* and the tone completely changes. Why not read Scripture that way?

One Christmas Eve a young associate pastor was asked to be the liturgist for the service of lessons and carols. Between each of the nine carols, he was to read an assigned Bible passage having to do with the birth of Jesus. He decided this was a great opportunity to experiment with tone. So he changed his presentation from the usual flatness to that of a fatherly narrator reading bedtime stories to his children. Afterward, to his astonishment, several people asked him, "What were those beautiful readings between the songs? Did you write those?" While it was a sad testimony to how unfamiliar his congregants were with the Scriptures, it was a classic example of how a change in tone can radically alter our engagement with God's Word. By reading the Bible as an enchanting story, he had allowed the Scriptures to be strange and beautiful again. The congregation responded as if hearing the story for the first time.

Of course, what we've said about the Bible in worship also applies to Christian education and the home. Let's consider Christian education. For instance, what do we want our children to say when we ask, "What did you learn in Sunday school?" Many times they'll answer, "We learned about sharing," or "We learned to be nice to people." This is called a moral lesson. Quite frankly, if that's all they learned, their teacher just as well could have told them the moral by itself—why bother with story at all? One could argue that we tack stories onto lessons because stories are useful for illustrating the point of the lesson; stories stick in the memory better than statements. True. But if the lesson is about sharing, why not teach "Goldilocks and the Three Bears"? Again, one could argue that we want our children to become familiar with God's Word because that's how they become familiar with God. True again. And yet we must never forget that Bible stories do not exist to illustrate *some other point* God is trying to get across. Jesus is not merely *an example* of God's love: Jesus *is* God's love. The stories are the point. So when we ask, "What did you learn in Sunday school?" the answer we should be looking for is, "Once there was a man on his way from Jerusalem to Jericho. . . ."

To reduce a Bible story to nothing but a moral lesson limits the hearers' engagement with it on an imaginative level. It keeps them from stepping inside the story and walking around; from getting caught up in the action and feeling as the characters feel. It keeps them from seeing with a whole new perspective. To reduce a Bible story to a moral is to foreclose on what the hearers are supposed to "get out" of the text, as if there were no other meanings to be found. So instead of asking, "What is the point of the parable of the Good Samaritan?" perhaps we might ponder, "I wonder why the third man stopped?" or "I wonder how the victim felt when the priest and Levite passed him by?"[8]

Inviting a classroom of first graders—and adults!—to wonder about a Bible story can create teachable moments when the hearers are actually open and curious. They may ask wondering questions related to cultural context ("I wonder what a Samaritan is?"), at which point the teacher can pause and teach about biblical geography and history. Or they may ask wondering questions about racial prejudice, at which point the teacher can bring in theological claims about how all humans are made in the image of God. This is where the responses of the catechism are relevant. It's not the doctrines or beliefs that come first, but the stories of Scripture. The responses of the catechism make sense only in light of those stories. So it's not that we avoid teaching or instruction when engaging the Bible as story. Instead we begin with the story, and our instruction flows organically out of the wondering and curiosity of the hearers.

The Bible anticipates this kind of wondering, especially at home among families. As we've already noted, at various points throughout the Old Testament parents are told to *expect* questions from their children, and they're commanded to tell God's story in response. Take the book of Joshua. After God parts the waters so the Israelites can cross over the Jordan River into the promised land, they are instructed to make a pile of stones as a sign of what God has done. "When your children ask in time to come, 'What do these stones mean to you?' then you shall tell them that the waters of the Jordan were cut off in front of the ark of the covenant of the LORD. . . . So these stones shall be to the Israelites a memorial forever" (Josh. 4:6-7). The episode echoes an earlier injunction in Deuteronomy 6:6-7: "Keep these words that I am commanding you today in your heart. Recite them to your children and talk about them when you are at home and when you are away, when you lie down and when you rise." Biblical storytelling is not limited to worship or Sunday school: it starts and ends at home.

But what fun! As commandments go, this one is delightful: we get to tell stories. And it's user-friendly: presenting the story of Scripture does not take special theological training or technological gizmos. The words are there in the book, beautiful and eloquent in their simplicity, often mysterious, occasionally complex, but ours, by God's grace. This is our story, a living story, like the ones our grandparents told when we were small children. The words don't need to be adorned with extra details, ramped up with special effects and subwoofers, or made hilarious and quirky with cartoon animation. They don't need to be dressed up with modern lingo in order to sound hip and relevant ("Dude!" said Johnny the Baptistorama, "How'd you get the 411 on the wrath to come?"). They speak a language all their own, the language of faith; and we want these phrases and sentences, images, and themes to become deeply embedded in who we are. It starts by resisting the "off" switch when the Word is read and proclaimed on a Sunday morning. And it continues as we pay attention to narrative tone and create space

The Bible is a world inviting us in. Indeed it is a normative world—which is to say, it offers a way of life that trumps all the other stories of this world. The things we learn during our encounters with Scripture come not by memorizing some kind of point or moral lesson about it, but by letting it shape our desires and fears, hopes and actions. We live so long inside these stories that our own lives take on a biblical shape. Eventually we come to know the biblical story so well that we recognize the episodes we find ourselves in—we can distinguish dragons (and Samaritans) when we see them. Most importantly, we develop the instincts to act in story-formed ways. A pastor once told his congregation about the Sunday morning he was late to church. He was bombing down the road in the pouring rain with his children in the backseat when they passed a woman whose car had broken down. One of his kids asked, "Aren't we going to stop?" He replied, "No, honey, we're already late to church." A few moments passed. Then a small voice from the backseat said, "I sure hope someone comes by who doesn't have to go to church." Needless to say, the pastor turned around. Worship started late that day.

Our Lord knows that even if we memorize all the kings of Judah—their exports, imports, governments, and drains (water being an important resource in the desert, of course)—we still could be no better equipped than Eustace to face the dragons. It's not the Bible as encyclopedia that shapes us, but the Bible as story. It's the story that teaches us to love the right things, to dream the right things, to practice the right things. Eventually, in our congregations, classrooms, and homes, we will—by God's grace—live lives worthy of the story in which we find ourselves.

Recommended Resources

- *Book, Bath, Table, and Time: Worship as Source and Resource for Youth Ministry* by Fred Edie (Pilgrim Press, 2007)

- *Desiring the Kingdom: Worship, Worldview, and Cultural Formation* by James K. A. Smith (Baker, 2009)

- *The God-Hungry Imagination: The Art of Storytelling for Postmodern Youth Ministry* by Sarah Arthur (Upper Room Books, 2007)

- *Godly Play: An Imaginative Approach to Christian Education* by Jerome Berryman (Augsburg, 1991)

- *How to Read the Bible as Literature . . . and Get More Out of It* by Leland Ryken (Zondervan, 1985)

- *The Literary Study Bible,* ed. Leland and Philip Ryken (Crossway Bibles, 2007)

- *Shaped by the Story: Helping Students Encounter God in a New Way* by Michael Novelli (Youth Specialties, 2008)

- *The True Story of the Whole World* by Michael Goheen and Craig Bartholomew (Faith Alive Christian Resources, 2009)

Chapter 4

"It's What We Do":
Faith Formation at Home

Elizabeth F. Caldwell

It's Saturday night. A family with teenage boys sits down for dinner. Two of the boys' friends join them for the family meal. Hands reach out and join for the blessing the family has been singing together ever since the boys were in preschool. One of the friends, a regular dinner guest at this table, has learned the blessing. "It's what we do," the mother explains to the other friend.

It's what we do! We say thank you to God for health and strength and food to eat. Some people talk about the important role of parents in helping their children "find faith" at home. But I believe the real issue is not so much *finding* faith at home as it is *living* the faith at home. It's essential for Christians to make connections between the faith practices we experience at church (prayer, reading and studying the Bible, caring for others, exploring ways to live faithfully and responsibly in the world) and living these practices at home.

Most Christians affirm the idea that growing in faith is both supported and challenged by active participation in the life and witness of a congregation. Yet this alone is not adequate. Parents and extended family members are *partners* with the congregation in forming faith. They are faith educators whose Christian identity nurtures and supports faithful living in the world.

How do parents and families function as faith educators? Nurturing children in the Christian faith requires immersing families in spiritual practices at home. Parents' commitment to the spiritual formation of their children is strengthened when they participate together in such practices as praying, listening for what God is saying, reflecting on life and how it connects with faith, seeing the world through the lens of faith, meditating, reading Scripture, and caring for others. Such experiences connect children, youth, and adults to the holy, to the mysteries of God, and to practical ways of caring for neighbors—all of which strengthens their Christian identity.

Yes . . . But: Realities and Challenges

Three underlying realities or tensions serve as background for understanding both the challenges and possibilities for connecting faith and the home. They can be framed by the following statements.

Maybe you've even said them yourself, or heard them from a friend.

- *Yes*, I'm a Christian, *but* isn't it the job of my church to teach my children?

- *Yes*, I know it's important to make time to read my Bible and pray and help a neighbor in need, *but* it's so hard to find the time, and honestly, I don't where or how to begin.

- *Yes*, I want to continue to grow in my life as a Christian and I want to help my children grow up with some practices of faith that will grow with them as they age, *but* I need some ideas for how to do this.

One challenge to the notion of the role of family in Christian formation is the attitude that it takes *professional knowledge and expertise*. Most Protestant congregations share a similar model of religious education. Sunday is the day for worship and Christian education (separated by age groups), and church school is the primary context where children and youth learn the content of the Christian faith and make connections between that content and the practice of living as a Christian in the world. But that model raises the obvious question, "What about the days between Sundays?"

Some congregations offer a variety of additional contexts for learning: midweek gatherings, Sunday evening services, retreats, vacation Bible school, mission trips, and church camps. Many also have strong mission commitments within their communities and offer opportunities for families to participate together in ministry with people who are homeless, with tutoring programs, and with programs that provide care for young children and older adults. By participating together in such activities, people of all ages learn that the Christian faith is lived out in the world.

Yet increasingly we leave the task of raising children and teenagers in faith, of nurturing their spirituality, to the "professionals"—pastors and church educators. As a result, "Children grow up biblically illiterate in homes where Bibles abound but are rarely opened. We have become a generation incapable of passing on the stories of our faith. The face of our faith has become extremely impoverished. Instead of being rich banquets, feasts of faith and community, our tables of faith have become barren with barely enough bread and water to satisfy, and we try to sustain ourselves on this meager diet."[1]

Martin Marty, a distinguished church historian and observer of culture, has said that most American Christians "are woefully unprepared to be responsible agents of their faith. They know too little of its story, its teaching, and its moral framework to exemplify and testify to their faith in a pluralist culture. So they blend into the culture or are overwhelmed by it or desert the faith for one or another of the options in it."[2]

So in response to that first "yes . . . but," it's not enough just to get to church on Sunday. Those days *between* Sundays—when life happens and we struggle to make connections with our faith and find answers for some of the difficult questions that arise—are just as important for growing faith.

The second "yes . . . but" challenge raises the question of *time and ability*. Because of busy work schedules and after-school activities, many families find it difficult even to sit down together for a meal. A real issue in our culture is our concept of time: *kairos* (Sabbath time) versus *chronos* time. Our culture lives by the clock; it values speed and change. In some ways time has become our most cherished possession. That attitude spills over into the church as well; for example, when congregations schedule church school for children and youth at the same time as worship "because parents want it all done in one hour—that's all the time they have." In contrast, many Korean, Hispanic, and African American congregations live by God's *kairos* time. Gathering for worship is a time to be in community with each other and with God, to support and care for one another.

We all live by *chronos* time, and yet we are all called to live into *kairos* time. If we live only by the clock, constantly checking our cell phones for new text messages and emails, what happens to the time we spend with God?

Spirituality is not something we need to add into an already full schedule. Rather, it is being attuned to the mystery and wonder of God's presence in our daily lives. Jean Grasso Fitzpatrick has observed that "a spiritual life is not something we begin to lead—or to cultivate in our children—after analyzing every book in the Bible, or resolving to be do-gooders, or even deciding we believe in God. Spirit is our life's breath . . . Spirituality is not something we need to pump into our children, as though it were nitrous oxide at the dentist. Like oxygen, it is freely available to each of us at every moment of life. Spirit is in every breath we draw and so is spiritual nurture."[3]

Finally, many churchgoing Christians admit that they want to grow in their life as a Christian, but *they don't know where or how to begin*. Perhaps they grew up in homes where they didn't learn any spiritual practices. Or they want to try some new things but they don't know how to begin. In some two-parent families, only one parent is a Christian, and so that parent struggles with the singular job of nurturing children's faith at home.

Here is a place where the church needs to focus on preparing and supporting adults for their vocation as faith educators. Too often church leaders assume that parents know how to raise their children in the Christian faith, and so they fail to provide opportunities to learn about simple Christian practices or rituals for the home, either in classes or in informal conversation.

In sharp contrast to a culture that places a high value on individualism and looking out for oneself, the Christian faith relies on the formative power of community. So, for example, the sacrament of baptism takes place in the context of worship, when the people of faith gather around the individual or the family. Bonnie Miller-McLemore writes that it is time for congregations to discuss "the radical understanding of parenting as a religious discipline and community practice"; she believes that "the practice of raising children belongs to all Christians, and not solely to parents or to mothers."[4]

What support structures are necessary for parents and extended family members to grow in their own faith and to help them nurture their children and teens in the life of the Christian faith? What areas of spiritual formation need the most attention in the home? Is it possible for congregations to consider a new model of religious education, one that supports the spiritual formation of parents and supports them in their role as faith educators? Can we turn the "yes . . . but," into "I can, and I will"? I believe we can, if we are willing to take on the vocation of making a home for faith in our lives.

Making a Home for Faith

So where and how do adults begin or continue this lifelong vocation of faith formation? We can think about this question by focusing on three roles: *translator, partner*, and *connector.*

First, adults need to function in their homes as *translators* of the faith. Parents who are able to use biblical vocabulary such as *sin, grace*, and *forgiveness*; who are able to talk about God's work as creator and God's self-revelation in Jesus; who can translate difficult theological concepts such as providence or redemption in simple terms like "God's plans for a good world" or "God loves you even when you do something wrong" are giving their children a language of faith that helps them *experience* faith even before they *understand* the language that describes it.

Many congregations give children a story Bible or a student Bible at important points in their life such as baptism, completing second or third grade (when most children can read on their own), or graduation. Congregations also need to educate parents about the importance of reading, meditating on, and being at home with the Bible, so that children can grow in their ability to translate their beliefs into faithful living in the world.

Helping children understand differences of culture, language, abilities, race, or faith is another important faith practice. In creation, God pronounced it all "good." Immersion in the stories of Scripture surrounds children like the waters of their baptism and prepares them for times when they have questions about the faith. Parents and extended family members who feel comfortable in their own "religious skin," so to speak, will not be paralyzed by questions from their children or critical challenges from their teens or young adults.

A second role adults need to take on is that of *partner* with the congregation in educating children in the faith. Such partnership means that congregations will seek practical ways—through education, worship, and mission opportunities—to help people of all ages understand the importance of caring for children. It means that congregations enable adults of all ages, together as a community, to love and care for children. And it means that adults of all ages understand that caring for children is a religious discipline, a response to our commitment at their baptism.

At the same time, if Christian families are to thrive in a multi-faith culture, parents must accept their calling as primary faith educators for their children. Faith that is alive and active in the home has a biblical basis in both the Old and New Testaments. Deuteronomy 6:4-9 represents a concise but deeply meaningful statement about the relationship between humankind and God: "Hear, O Israel: The LORD our God, the LORD is one. Love the LORD your God with all your heart and with all your soul and with all your strength." The writer goes on to say that these commandments must be kept in our hearts and impressed on our children. We are to recite them both at home and away from home. This affirmation of our faith in God should also be visible in the world: "Write them on the doorframes of your houses and on your gates."

Matthew records the words of Jesus, who, when his disciples asked him which commandments were the most important, responded with the words of Deuteronomy and then added a second commandment: "Love your neighbor as yourself" (Matt. 22:39). So our thankful response to God's presence in our lives is to love God and love others as ourselves.

In addition to our role as *translators* and *partners* with the church in faith formation, we have a third role: to *connect the biblical story with faithful living in the world.* Parents, grandparents, aunts, or uncles can help children and teens make connections between their faith and the world in which they live. Having heard the great commandment to love God and to love our neighbors as ourselves, we need to reflect on what that means for our daily living.

A primary way for congregations to partner with adults in their role of helping kids make connections between their faith and daily living is to provide opportunities for families to practice their faith. For example, churches can offer workshops for families based on the seasons of the Christian year—Advent, Christmas, Epiphany, Lent, Holy Week, Easter, Pentecost, and Ordinary Time. During Advent, the church could provide time and space for families to come together and make Advent wreaths or calendars. Before Ash Wednesday, it could suggest ways for families to mark the forty days of Lent.

In our role as connectors, we understand how faith practices help tune our hearts to the mystery and wonder of God's presence in our lives. Craig Dykstra has identified thirteen such practices that he believes are important for Christians today: worship, telling the Christian story, interpreting Scripture, prayer, confession of sin and reconciliation, encouraging others, acts of service and witness, suffering with neighbors, providing hospitality and care, listening, struggling to understand the context of life, criticizing and resisting the powers of evil, and working together to create social structures that sustain life in accord with God's will.[5]

All of these practices are examples of the kinds of spiritual practices that can shape a family's rituals of faith at home and that support church participation. A family can make commitments to growing in grace through participating in worship, reading and interpreting the biblical story, and praying. Some ancient Christian practices offer simple ways to begin. *Lectio divina,* for example, involves hearing or reading Scripture three times, each time listening for something different: a word, an image, the way that God is speaking to you in this text. The *Examen* is a way of reflecting on the activities of the day in terms of "consolations" and "desolations, asking questions such as "When did you receive God's love today?" "When did you share God's love today?" Some parents like to use this kind of reflection at the dinner table with kids, using the terms "sads" and "glads." The *Examen* is also a great way to close the day before sleep. Walking labyrinths during Lent is another simple Christian practice that helps people of all ages engage in meditative prayer.

Congregational worship provides opportunities for everyone to experience and pray different kinds of prayers: adoration, confession, thanksgiving, and supplication or intercession for others (sometimes called ACTS). You can also try praying some of these kinds of prayers at home with your children. Or try a breath prayer, something you can say in one breath. Marc Gellman and Thomas Hartman believe it's easy to teach children to pray different kinds of prayers: "thanks, gimme, wow, and oops"—prayers of thanksgiving, supplication, adoration, and confession.[6]

And don't forget the simple Christian practice of learning how to stop and be still, to listen for God and connect with the mystery and wonder of God's world.

Families practice acts of love and mercy when they encourage and serve others, stand alongside neighbors who are suffering, provide hospitality, or care for each other. In writing about the moral teaching of adults, Robert Coles points out that what is important for children is "the witness of our lives, our ways of being with others and speaking to them and getting on with them—all of that taken in slowly, cumulatively, by our sons and daughters, our students. . . . in the long run of a child's life, the unself-conscious moments that are what we think of simply as the unfolding events of the day and the week turn out to be the really powerful and persuasive times morally."[7]

The simplicity of these spiritual practices that define "acts of mercy" is astounding. They are the activities we engage in every day, no matter what our age. Naming them and helping children and teens connect with them are important. When parents are transparent, letting their children see the ordinary acts of faith they do every day, those children grow up with an identity of faith.

The call to be formed spiritually stands in sharp contrast to the call of the world to accumulate possessions and to buy the latest technology. Christians live with the tension between the call of the culture and the call of Jesus to feed those who are hungry and thirsty, to care for those who are sick or in prison, to welcome the stranger (Matt. 25:31-46). Our faith practices lead to and connect with our practice of mercy in the world.

Finally, Christians are called to practice acts of justice—to create structures in our communities and in our country that are in accord with God's will. Families who engage in table conversations about what's happening in the world and in the community, who talk about places where God's presence is needed, are equipping their children to discern, criticize, and form judgments about how to practice their faith in the world. And when families join their congregations in acts of justice such as serving meals to older adults or homeless shelter guests, building houses with Habitat for Humanity, or participating in a hunger walk, they are responding to Jesus' challenge in Matthew 25:40: "Whatever you did for one of the least of these brothers and sisters of mine, you did for me."

Spiritual practices, writes Craig Dykstra, "place people in touch with God's redemptive activity . . . put us where life in Christ may be made known, recognized, experienced, and participated in. They are means of grace, the human places in which and through which God's people come to faith and grow to maturity in faith."[8] Practices of piety, mercy, and justice, when woven together in the faithful acts of a family, help provide a tapestry of support for living in the world.

This is supported by research conducted by Robert Wuthnow about what it means to "grow up religious." Wuthnow conducted interviews over a three-year period with two hundred people. After listening to them tell stories about their childhood experiences, he came to the conclusion that "embedded practices are influential in religious development because they spin out webs of significance that richly connect people with the world around them." Contrary to those who believe that religious formation requires hours of catechetical instruction at church, Wuthnow's evidence revealed that children "assimilated religion more by osmosis than by instruction."[9] For families who intentionally raised their children in a faithful home, faith came to be experienced as a natural way of life.

As Lisa Sowle Cahill writes, "The Christian family is not the perfect family but one in which fidelity, compassion, forgiveness, and concern for others, even strangers are known. In striving to embody these virtues, however imperfect its success, a family lives in the presence of God and begins to transform its surroundings."[10]

Congregations strengthen the spiritual lives of children and youth by supporting adults and nurturing their role as faith educators. Families who practice their faith at home discover how each family member is spiritually nurtured in her or his own unique way. As they make commitments together to be involved in acts of justice, mercy, and kindness, families grow together in their faith and in their Christian presence in the world. This is truly the way to make a space for faith at home.

Chapter 5

Step by Step:
Faith Development and Faith Formation

Robert J. Keeley

This past winter our church decided to engage the congregation in a study of worship. We got a book for adults and teens to read and discuss on Sunday evenings, but since these were materials designed for adults, we realized that we needed something else for children. My wife, Laura, assembled some lessons on worship from a few other sources, and leaders of both adult and children's groups enjoyed the study.

In one of the sessions, Laura asked the children, ranging in ages from third to sixth grade, to think about special events in their lives and place them on a time line. The children wanted to list things like "one-year-old birthday," "two-year-old birthday," and so on. Laura was looking for something else, so she said, "What about the first time you rode a bike or maybe when your baby brother was born?" But even with the examples Laura gave, kids just couldn't do the task she was asking them to do. Afterward, as we thought about it together, we realized that we were seeing developmental theory in action. Kids of this age have a difficult time seeing that they have a personal past and a personal future. They can't see the big picture very well yet. As they grow older they'll be able to do that, but they can't do it yet.

It was a good reminder of the importance of thinking about development in issues of faith formation and church ministry. It is very easy for us to think of development in terms of physical tasks: we'd never ask a two-year-old to ride a two-wheeled bike without training wheels because we know kids that age don't yet have the balance to do that. But sometimes we don't think about other types of development and what impact that information might have on how we do things.

There are many types of development and a number of theories about how people progress through various developmental stages: theories of physical development, cognitive development (how we think), psychosocial development (how we interact with others), moral development, and also faith development. As we think about faith formation, it is useful to think about what impact development might have on the way people interact with our ministry.

Much of what we know about faith development comes from the work of John Westerhof and James Fowler. Their theories of faith development are useful (although imperfect) tools to help us understand what we might expect as people grow in their faith. Both theories cover much of the same territory, but in this chapter we'll focus on Fowler's theory.

Before we begin, though, there are a few things that we should keep in mind.

First of all, faith is from God; it is the result of the Holy Spirit's work in our lives. Turning it into series of stages through which we navigate is at best tricky and at worst a complete misrepresentation of the mystery and wonder of God's presence in our lives. So we need to remind ourselves continuously that faith development is nothing without the Holy Spirit's guidance.

Second, this theory is flawed. What's more, we don't know exactly how it's flawed. So we need to be really careful when we apply this information. Fowler's theory has been criticized for being based on Western Christianity and for not being as universal a theory of faith development as he claims. So perhaps what Fowler says doesn't apply as well to Christians from non-Western cultures. Fowler's faith development theory is based on the developmental theories of Jean Piaget, Erik Erikson, and Lawrence Kohlberg, all of which also have limitations.

Finally, all developmental theories recognize that although the order in which we move from stage to stage is fairly consistent, the amount of time each person spends in each stage varies quite a bit. It's like the way children learn how to walk: we can say the general order in which things happen, but we really can't tell when they're going to happen. We need to resist the urge to think of these developmental stages as discrete—instead there is a gradual change from one stage to the next.

Having made all those disclaimers, it might seem that we can hardly say anything at all about how we develop faith, but that's not quite true either. It's been my experience, and the experience of others, that these stages of faith ring true, and that thinking about them gives us insight into how we and others develop in our faith. So let's look at Fowler's theory[1] and consider what we can learn from it about how people in various stages can be nurtured in their faith.

In his book *Stages of Faith*, Fowler considers the faith of very young children—up to age two—a "pre-stage" he calls *undifferentiated faith*. This is a stage in which we form our first pre-images of God. While we don't specifically learn about God in this stage, the things we learn set the stage for what will come later. Ministry to children at this age, therefore, should be about the very things we would expect—care and safety. The best thing we can do for children this age is to give them a place where they are well cared for when their parents are in worship or in meetings, and where both they and their parents feel comfortable.

The next stage of faith, which Fowler refers to as the first stage, is *intuitive-projective faith*. This stage is found primarily in preschool children and is primarily a reflection of parental faith. It would be easy to conclude that this isn't really a child's own faith. But that conclusion misses an important point: children of this age are generally unable to think abstractly, to take someone else's perspective on things, or to think through complex ideas.[2] Their faith is not a "thought-out" faith. So it would be unrealistic to expect children of this age to give any logical or well-organized description of their faith. Their faith talk will reflect their thoughts—it will be based on impressions and stories they have picked up by being around people of faith in their home and at church.

Knowing that children of this age are building a foundation for the type of faith they experience later, we want to be careful about the impressions we give them at this early age. Kids learn stories from us in church, but they also learn other things that might have an even larger impact, such as the climate of the church. They'll quickly pick up a sense of whether church is a place where they feel comfortable.

Children this age also like a certain amount of repetition. When our kids were younger they had their favorite audiotapes, videos, and DVDs. In the case of our youngest child we saw more episodes of *Barney* than we could possibly enjoy, but our daughter continued to watch them. We saw an example of this at church a few years back. In our children's worship center for three-year-olds, we began each Sunday by playing with Play-Doh. We saw this as a way to help children settle down and get acclimated to the leader and to each other. We did this each week, and the children seemed to like it. One summer we decided to change things up a bit. We asked all the children ages three through third grade to come to a different room and listen to a story together. The three-year-olds were not happy. A few of them just couldn't figure out why we had changed things—they wanted their Play-Doh time! This reminded us just how important repetition and ritual are for children.

To help children of this age grow in their faith, repetition should happen not just in children's worship rooms but also in congregational worship and in their homes. For example, perhaps congregational worship could include certain songs that are sung every week (such as the Doxology) or words of blessing that are repeated from week to week. At home families might establish mealtime rituals involving prayers, sung blessings, or Scripture reading. These are things young children can grab on to, and they will come to expect them every day or every week.

As preschoolers get older they move into Fowler's next stage of development, *mythic-literal faith*. This is the elementary school stage: it is found in children starting at around age six, and it ofte lasts until age eleven or twelve. These children can articulate ' faith better than they could before, but that has as much to language development as it does with faith developm children's faith is still primarily a reflection of their their world has gotten bigger, and people outsi' also have significant influence on their faith.

I remember when my oldest daughter was in kindergarten. One evening at dinner I asked her to lead us in a prayer at the end of our meal. She prayed a prayer similar to the ones I had prayed at the table since she was old enough to pay attention, but then she added a request for one of her classmates who was sick. That struck me because it was the first time I noticed her faith being influenced by someone other than my wife or me. She was imitating what her Christian school teacher had done in class. She demonstrated in a small way what Fowler suggests happens ordinarily at this stage.

Children in this stage learn more and more of the stories of the Old and New Testaments. Kids begin to connect these stories together, but they still aren't quite ready to see them as part of one large story. Story is important to all of us in our faith formation, but it is especially important to children at this age. For one thing, stories catch their attention. This is true for all of us, of course (see ch. 3), but it is especially true for these children because they are not good with abstract concepts yet. This makes stories particularly well suited to them, as opposed to lessons about God or about how our faith is organized. Even more important, stories give these children a sense of who they are and what it means to be the people of God. These are our family stories, and learning them is important at this stage in faith development. It gives children the building blocks they'll need to begin putting things together when they get to the next stage of development.

The church, then, has a wonderful opportunity to share the important stories of faith with children at a time when they are developmentally ready to receive them. A dry transmission of these stories isn't going to do it, though. We need to use this opportunity to share these stories with them in a way that allows children to live inside of the stories.[3] If instead we use stories as a vehicle to get to a moral lesson, we are merely giving children a checklist of do's and don'ts instead of introducing them to the stories of God and his people.

In his book *Faith Is a Verb*, Kenneth Stokes writes that this stage is also present in some adults. He writes that adults who possess a faith that is "straightforward and literalistic" experience their faith this way.[4] These people will likely find themselves most comfortable in a church that emphasizes a highly literal interpretation of Scripture and a strong sense of the authority of church leaders. While they will not have the same cognitive restrictions as elementary school children, they may come to their faith in the same unexamined way.

The next stage, *synthetic-conventional faith*, begins around the time students enter middle school and lasts throughout much of high school. Again, some people may remain in this stage for much of their lives. Anyone who has spent much time with middle schoolers knows that identity formation is a big part of what is happening at this time. Piaget's theory of cognitive development suggests that children in this stage are beginning to be able to handle abstraction. This has a number of ramifications in education as well as other areas. For example, these children and teens more fully realize that they have a personal past and a personal future. They are also capable of seeing things from the perspective of other people—a skill they often use to look at themselves. This fuels the self-absorption—sometimes called adolescent egocentrism—that we see in kids this age. Describing life with their teenage son, friends of ours said it was like "Caleb Radio—all Caleb, all the time." Because adolescents see the world through the relatively new lens of imagining what others think, they spend an inordinate amount of time thinking about themselves.

Self-absorption is not the only issue in this stage, of course. Because they are more capable of abstract thought, kids this age are beginning to put the Bible stories they have been hearing for years into a larger story of faith. They can, for example, begin to understand the connections between the Exodus, the celebration of the Passover, and the Lord's Supper. These connections, which help us realize that the Bible is one large story, are difficult for younger children to understand.

Two other interesting things are also going on at this time: a desire for independence and a strong desire to belong to a group. Since teens at this stage want to be independent, they are at the point where they want to choose their own faith. For the first time, their faith is not merely a reflection of someone else's faith. They actually make some deliberate personal commitments. Since their experience is quite limited, though, and they still want to be part of a group, for the most part they choose the faith of their parents. So even though they make a choice, the list of options is usually limited to one—the faith they were raised in.

Sometimes teens literally wear their identities on their sleeves—you can often tell how they identify themselves based on the way they dress. Recently my wife and I passed two teenage boys who were pretty clearly communicating a few things about themselves without saying anything. The way they had their hair and the way they dressed identified them with a particular group of teens in our community who spend their free time skateboarding. Whether they realized it or not, these boys had carefully crafted an image that identified them as part of the skater group. To a certain extent, this is true of all teens: all teens are working on their identities, and they often begin by identifying themselves with (or against) certain groups.

Another important issue in this stage and the next is the location of authority. For young children, authority is clearly located with their parents. Parents have control over many of their decisions, certainly the big ones. But as children grow into teens and then into young adults, the location of that authority shifts from being primarily external (with parents) to primarily internal. People in Fowler's *synthetic-conventional faith* stage of faith, whether they are teens or much older, give over much of the authority for their faith to someone else. Cult leaders use this sort of authority structure to help them control the people who follow them. And Christian leaders who see themselves as having God-given authority over their flock may structure their church in a synthetic-conventional mode. They may care deeply for their followers, but depend on them to pretty much do what they say.

In contrast, the fourth stage, *individuative-reflective faith*, is characterized by what happens when people take control of their faith. In this stage the authority for an individual's faith resides within that person instead of with someone else. Again, this shift in the center of authority doesn't happen overnight. But changes such as moving away from home—perhaps moving away to begin college or start a job—can initiate the beginning of such a shift or make it happen more quickly.

People in this stage examine their faith in a way they really didn't before. They take a step back from the faith they accepted when they were younger and begin to ask if it really works for them. They allow themselves to engage questions that may have been lurking under the surface for a while.

This isn't just a phase for college students and other young adults, although a number of students find themselves here. Research has found that this stage happens for different people throughout their adult lives. People in this stage are allowing questions to have a foothold in their faith. This can be a powerfully positive experience, especially when they have the opportunity to work through their questions with someone who listens carefully, thinks through the questions with them, and explores the beginnings of answers. It doesn't take a theologian to know that God is bigger than we can imagine, and it makes sense that there will be questions for which we just don't have answers. Some people, according to Kenneth Stokes, are told simply not to question their faith.[5] This sort of response is never helpful. People in this stage aren't going to be satisfied with a "because I told you so" kind of faith—they want something they can grapple with.

People in this stage of faith seek a church community that allows them to express their faith in their own way. At this point their faith is quite individualistic; for the first time, their faith belongs to them as a person instead of to them as a group. A few years back I was talking to a student who told me that she had her own personal beliefs that didn't match any church or organized group. Back then I found it remarkable that a person of this age could assume that her nineteen years of experience gave her insights that centuries of thought by thousands of people hadn't come up with! But really she was simply giving voice to what this stage is all about. She needed to define her faith in her own way. It needed to make sense to her, and accepting someone else's answers wasn't going to cut it.

What we sometimes see in this stage of faith—and what I saw in that student—is a throwing off of the trappings of church—a desire to reinvent faith to get at the heart of "what really counts." This might involve switching to a church that is perceived as "alive" or "authentic." It might mean getting involved more deeply in church education. It might mean staying in the same church but seeking additional places to grow in faith, perhaps by attending a Bible study at another church, attending outside lectures and worship services, or reading books that speak to the person's individual expressions of faith. Of course, other factors also enter into these decisions. Relationships formed over the years, for example, may keep people in their churches even if they don't feel that their needs are being met. But many people come to a time when their previously unexamined faith gets put under the microscope.

Churches can respond to this stage of faith in a preemptive way by presenting the Christian faith to children in a way that invites their questions. We want to give children a faith that shows that we grapple with Scripture and seek to discover God's will for our lives.

In stage five, which Fowler calls *conjunctive faith,* the unsettled feelings that characterize stage four seem to settle down. People in this stage can own the faith of the community in a way they couldn't before. There are still questions, but these arise in the context of a solid faith. There is a strong sense that "my faith" has become "our faith." People in this stage recognize the depth and richness of long-standing expressions of faith and are ready to embrace them. They may be ready for significant encounters with Christian faith traditions other than their own. But unlike an earlier stage, in which people may try out other ways of doing things to see if they fit, this time they may be searching for insights that can enrich their own faith. In this stage of faith, people are not afraid to recognize the wisdom of others with regard to faith. Fowler cautions that this is not a "wishy-washy neutrality"[6]—instead it represents someone who is open to other perspectives because he or she is extremely well grounded in faith.

People in this stage of faith are often eager for insights that can give them a richer and fuller understanding of God and God's work in the world. These people will be open to in-depth teaching and service opportunities as well as opportunities to work with other churches and faith groups while remaining deeply engaged in their home church. They are able to see the beauty of worship that is both progressive and ancient. They can see the complex in the simple. They can be part of a group without feeling like they are sacrificing their individuality.

Fowler adds a sixth stage, *universalizing faith*, to his list, which we'll briefly mention here. This stage, according to Fowler, is a radical living out of your faith. The faith that has been solidified in stage five has an even greater impact on the life of a believer. Fowler says this stage is quite rare; he mentions examples such as Mother Teresa or Martin Luther King, Jr.

We should keep a few things specifically in mind when we think about faith development and faith formation:

- It is important to articulate our faith to each other and to our children. In their book *Soul Searching*, Smith and Denton write that "religious language is like any other language: to learn to speak it, one needs first to listen to native speakers using it a lot, and then one needs plenty of practice speaking it oneself."[7] We get better at understanding our faith by articulating it, and we articulate it better when we practice. So giving children and others religious language will help in their overall development.

- Bible stories are vitally important in helping children (and all of us) understand that our faith is much more than just a series of rules or moral lessons. God introduces himself to us in these stories, and they help us know him and know ourselves. They are our family stories.

- People of all ages need to know they have an important place in the church community. One way to do that is to give them an opportunity to lead in worship. Senior citizens, young children, and everyone in between should feel that the majority of church programs give them an opportunity to rub shoulders with each other. Having adults in the lives of younger Christians is good for everyone. Children learn that the faith that they received from their parents is shared by other important people as well; they get a first-hand look at how older Christians live their lives; and they see that *all* of church life—not just the "kids' part"—is for them. Older adults get to share their personal stories and they get to practice articulating their faith. They're also reminded that the questions raised by teens and young adults are an important part of the faith journey.

- The home is vitally important to the early years of faith development. Not only do children and teens spend more time at home than anywhere else, but the influence of parents on early faith development is hard to overemphasize. Churches should support parents as they help their children learn about God and his work in their lives.

- All of these stages are best experienced in community. By being with other Christians in various stages of faith development, we have the chance to more fully experience our own faith. We were created to live in community, and it is in community that our faith can grow best and find its best expression. Giving children a strong sense of the Christian community is the best way to give them the support they need in the various stages of their faith.

Chapter 6

Liturgy for a Lifetime: Faith Formation through Worship

Robbie Fox Castleman

I recall looking at my young husband in horror the first time he ordered fried catfish in a southern restaurant. As a transplant from the west coast, I'd grown up under the wise teaching of my father, who opined, "Catfish are garbage fish—either throw them back or use them for bait." How could my husband not know this?

Habits shape our lives for good or ill.

The subtle rhythms of our life are often unexamined or misunderstood because "that's how it is" or "it's always been that way." One newlywed may say to his or her partner, "I like to fold undershirts like this" as they settle into new household habits. Or a toddler may lament, "Mom, you skipped a page!" during an abbreviated bedtime story. Our lives are shaped by lifelong patterns of unconsciously learned behavior. And these patterns are hard to change. Counselors help people break a bad habit by coaching them to disrupt everyday benign habits: to minimize the temptation for that after-dinner cigarette or dessert, eat in a different place with different dishes and leave the table immediately.

Life is liturgy. Life has patterns that shape us more and for a lot longer than we ever realize. It is no wonder that liturgy—the patterns of corporate worship—shapes our faith formation more than we ever realize. One of the reasons people wage "worship wars" is because people like what they like because they like it the way they like it! Worship wars aren't usually waged over the biblical understanding of God. Instead they focus on topics like the style of church music, how communion is served, or whether or not the pastor should wear a robe. This focus on the external styles of liturgy often keeps us from noticing the rhythm of a liturgy that really does shape our faith, life, and understanding of God. Changes in liturgical style are often surprisingly uncomfortable because they touch something deeper, and perhaps unconscious, concerning the shape of our faith.

In terms of style, corporate worship services can be quite distinct. However, nearly all congregations that have any sort of intentional connection with the historical faith formation and worship development of the early church follow a pattern of worship that

emerges in the Old and New Testaments. The patterns of the
historical liturgy underscore several ideas that are vital for the
worship of God and for forming biblical faith in congregations and
in the lives of believers.

God's Pleasure Is the Focus of Worship

David's words "Praise the LORD, my soul; all my inmost being, praise
his holy name" (Ps. 103:1) express the goal of biblical worship. The
pleasure, blessing, and glory of God should be the heartfelt desire
of God's people throughout worship. It's not about us! It's all about
God. We may be blessed in the long run, but this can never be our
goal if worship is a true expression of our love for God. Worship,
like true love, is a gift given with no strings attached. True love gives
itself for the simple pleasure of the other, not to coerce or manipulate
the other's love in return. If a man or woman gives a gift with the
intention of getting something in return, that is not true love but
self-love. True love knows nothing of payback, ulterior motives, or
a return on investment. Worship "in the Spirit and in truth" (John
4:24) is a congregational gift given simply as a response to being
loved first by God (1 John 4:19).

Called to Worship

Recognizing that worship is a loving response to the God who
loved us first fosters a sense of proper humility in the worshiping
community. God's people are called to worship. We assemble at
God's invitation, not our own initiative. The English word "worship"
is related to the word "worthy": to worship is to express that God
alone is worthy of glory, adoration, praise, allegiance, and sacrifice.
This recognition reminds us that apart from God's grace we are
unworthy people. Only by God's grace, through the person and
work of Jesus Christ, can we come to worship. Only through the
Son of God who has gone before us do we dare to approach the
throne of grace (Heb. 4:14-16).

A variety of symbols in congregational worship point to this
reality. Often the first act of worship is the lighting of candles,
indicating that Jesus has gone before us to call us to worship. We
enter the sanctuary to meet the God who is already present. Many

congregations use a responsive reading from Scripture as a call to worship, indicating that God's Word has called us to this hour. The pastor or worship leader might welcome the congregation, but it is God who has called us to assemble and who has gone before us as the mediator of all that is said and done.

Praise the Lord!

It should be no surprise that our first response to such grace is praise and adoration of the God who has called us to come. Who would not be thrilled at such an invitation? God's people are invited to join their voices with those who eternally sing "Holy, holy, holy" before the throne of God. John's account of heavenly visions in the book of Revelation gives us an idea of what we only glimpse in earthly worship: "Day and night they never stop saying: 'Holy, holy, holy is the Lord God Almighty, who was, and is, and is to come'" (4:8). And again, "You are worthy, our Lord and God, to receive glory and honor and power, for you created all things, and by your will they were created and have their being" (4:11).

Following this pattern, which is also mentioned in the Old Testament (Isa. 6:3), the first act after the antiphonal call to worship from the Scripture is a prayer of praise and the singing of songs that give glory to God.

Confession of Unworthiness

Recognizing God's ultimate worthiness and supreme glory also leads us to a stark awareness of our lack of personal and corporate worthiness to pray and sing such praise. Worshipers are rightly made aware that we all fall short of the glory of God (Rom. 3:23); left on our own, we are sinful, fallen people. In ancient Israel, confession of sin, even by the priests, was mandatory before offerings and sacrifices could be made. So in a service of worship modeled after the biblical pattern of Israel and the early church, the people confess their sin to God, both corporately and within their hearts. I don't know about you, but I always need more time for the silent confession of my own sin. The worship leader always seems to cut this time short with the "declaration of absolution." This declaration is the rehearsal of the gospel: the good news that because of Christ

Jesus and his final victory over sin and death in the resurrection, we are God's forgiven people.

The Declaration of God's Good News

Interrupting the confession of the sinner is actually quite biblical. That's exactly what the father of the wayward "prodigal son" did as his son headed for home (Luke 15:11ff.). Grace always interrupts our best efforts of contrition. Paul celebrates this in Romans 5:8: "God demonstrates his own love for us in this: While we were still sinners, Christ died for us." Our utter unworthiness is addressed by God's salvation through the life, suffering, death, resurrection, and ascension of Jesus Christ. "God, who is rich in mercy, made us alive with Christ even when we were dead in transgressions—it is by grace you have been saved. And God raised us up with Christ and seated us with him in the heavenly realms in Christ Jesus" (Eph. 2:4-6). Good news doesn't get any better than this. Is it any wonder that after the declaration of God's power to save that the congregation rises to sing some song of doxology? *Doxa* is the Greek root for the word "to praise"!

The Word of the Lord

As God's forgiven people, we hear the Word with hearts and ears cleansed anew by God's grace. This is the point in the service when passages from the Hebrew Scripture and the New Testament are read. Have you ever wondered why, in this time of high literacy, the Word of God is still read aloud for the whole congregation to hear? Certainly this is helpful for the very young, but there's more to this custom than its historical roots in the days when few people could read. Hearing God's Word spoken aloud in the congregation is a symbol that we are accountable to each other for acting on the Word we have heard together as God's people.

Jesus finished his Sermon on the Mount (Matt. 5-7) with this very idea. After teaching the Word of God, Jesus ended his sermon with the admonition that wisdom is the fruit of life for those who have heard his words and then obediently put them into practice (Matt. 7:24-27). Too often we think of Jesus' famous simile about the wise man who built his house upon a rock as just a cute children's song with hand motions. But this illustration is, in fact, the crescendo of Jesus' challenge to his congregation.

The hearing and preaching of God's Word in worship always follows the confession of sin and the declaration of God's grace in Christ Jesus. And it is always followed by the congregation responding to that Word together in a variety of ways.

Responding to God's Word

Obediently responding to the Word of God is a great joy in worship. We are initiated into the body of Christ and the community of the church in baptism. We sing songs that cement and celebrate the challenge of obedience to the Word we have just heard together. We signal our reconciliation and unity in Christ by blessing each other with the peace of Christ. We gather around the table of the Lord to rehearse the saving work of God in the broken body and shed blood of Christ Jesus. We share testimonies of faith and life as a way to honor God's faithfulness in our lives. And we present our tithes and offerings for the ongoing work of the congregation's witness and mission.

It is important to remember that in all the ways a congregation responds to God's Word, the focus is on God's glory and honor. The congregation's response is still intent on God's divine majesty. The gifts of God's Spirit as they are manifest in the congregation are offered in the service of God's pleasure through worship. Indeed, the congregation presents itself as a "living sacrifice, holy and pleasing to God—this is true worship" (Rom. 12:1).

It is also important to recognize that everything we do in a service of worship is a corporate gift to God, the stewardship of a community's life together in the Spirit. This is symbolized in a variety of ways. We place our money in a plate or basket in order to present the offering as the congregation's gift to God, not our own individual contribution. This corporate practice underscores that both the widow's mite and the wealthy person's tithe are offered as people who belong to each other through their belonging to God.

Congregations need to think biblically about why they do what they do in corporate worship, taking care not to lose the richness of historical patterns of worship that have shaped God's people. More is lost than we might realize when a box is placed in the back of the sanctuary as a receptacle for an individual's offering. Great theological richness and understanding are blotted out when the elements of the Lord's Supper are taken by individuals on their own initiative at any time instead of being served by the elders as a part of a communal meal instituted by Christ.

God calls his people to worship together. The congregation responds to God's gracious invitation with praise and thanksgiving, recognizing its sin and unworthiness to worship a holy God. The people's corporate confession of sin is interrupted by the good news of God's grace and the salvation secured for all God's people through the life, suffering, and work of God's Son. Together the congregation hears God's Word and responds in joyful obedience. All of these acts of worship are done for the glory and honor of God. And, then—wonder of wonders—the God we have blessed through our worship, turns around and blesses us!

The Benediction

Having responded to God's Word, God blesses us for the ongoing mission of his people. We are commissioned for the work and witness of the gospel in the name of the Father, Son, and Holy Spirit. The congregation is dismissed with God's blessing to be God's hands and feet and heart in the world. Worship gathers us together to bless God. And by God's grace, we receive the blessing of God to bear God's Spirit, together as the church, into a world that needs to hear and see and experience the presence of the God we have worshiped.

This seven-fold pattern marks worship in Scripture from Sinai to the exilic synagogue, from the early church to the Roman mass, from the liturgies of the Reformation to the frontier communities birthed through the Church's mission. From call to praise, from praise to confession, from confession to forgiveness, from forgiveness to the Word, from the Word to response, from response to benediction, the rhythm of biblical liturgy shapes our faith as the people of God. This rhythm is embedded in biblical narratives and in the whole canonical story of Scripture. One example from God's Word where this pattern is most evident is in Isaiah's experience of worship "in the year that King Uzziah died" (Isa. 6:1).

Isaiah 6: God's Liturgy

Pause for just a moment, put down this book, and get your Bible. Take some time to slowly and thoughtfully read the sixth chapter of Isaiah.

Then keep your Bible open to Isaiah 6 and resume reading this chapter. Notice the sequence of Isaiah's experience: it exactly follows the liturgy noted above in the outline of this chapter.

Verse 1: Isaiah is **called to worship.** Isaiah enters into the ongoing worship of God. The prophet's experience is initiated by God's grace, not by his own effort or attempt to manufacture a spiritual high or divine blessing. This is the only time in Scripture that an event is dated in relation to someone's death. "In the year that King Uzziah died" would have been a poignant reminder of a tragedy for Isaiah's first readers, along the lines of saying, "This happened on 9/11." Everyone knows where they were and what they were doing on 9/11. Or, if you are old enough, it's like recalling where you were when John F. Kennedy was assassinated. The "year that King Uzziah died" was a sad memory for Isaiah's readers because Uzziah had been a beloved king who ruled during a time of great prosperity and national achievement. For fifty-two years Uzziah was the king of Judah, the longest reign of any monarch of Israel or Judah. (You can read the story of Uzziah's great success in 2 Chronicles 26:1-15.)

Everyone also knew the circumstances of Uzziah's death. He died about two years after contracting a particularly virulent case of leprosy as divine judgment for trying to manufacture a spiritual experience in a way that was forbidden by God. (You can read all about it in 2 Chronicles 26:16-21.) As king of Judah, Uzziah was not a Levite, the tribe of Israel's priests. But he became proud (26:16) and decided he had earned the right to worship the Lord any way he wanted, even to go behind the curtain where only the Levites of the priesthood were allowed to go.

So when Isaiah wrote, "In the year that King Uzziah died, I saw the Lord seated on a throne" (Isa. 6:1), he knew his first readers would understand that Isaiah was called to and surprised by a worship experience far greater than the one Uzziah had tried to manufacture for himself.

Verses 2-3: Isaiah enters into the **praise** of God, which is led eternally by seraphs, "flaming ones." The next time the Greek translation of the word for "seraphs" is used is at Pentecost (Acts 2:3). The trifold "Holy, holy, holy" is fitting praise for the God who continues to reveals himself throughout Scripture as Father, Son, and Holy Spirit.

Verses 4-5: Isaiah becomes increasingly aware of his own unworthiness as he offers praise in God's presence. Isaiah makes a heartfelt **confession**, not just for his own sinfulness but for the sin of all God's people. How can he see God and continue to live? Only by God's grace.

Verses 6-7: God interrupts Isaiah's woe-filled confession. At God's initiative, the "flaming ones" bring the fire of divine atonement. The prophet's lips are cleansed so that he can hear the Word of God.

Verses 8-13: Isaiah hears the **Word of God**. God's Word to Isaiah is hard to hear: it is an invitation to a ministry of hardship and suffering. Unlike Uzziah, Isaiah will not be popular. Unlike Uzziah, Isaiah will not be considered successful. But also unlike Uzziah, Isaiah will prove himself faithful.

Verses 8, 11: As God speaks, Isaiah **responds** to God's call. He is willing to obey. And when the difficulties of God's call become clear, Isaiah struggles with its demands and asks what we would ask in Isaiah's place, "How long?"

Verse 13: At the end of this divine liturgy, God blesses Isaiah with this promise: "The holy seed will be the stump." Four chapters later, Isaiah relates, "A shoot will come up from the stump of Jesse" (11:1).

Embedded in the **benediction** of Isaiah 6 is the promise of the Son of David, the Messiah of Israel and the Alpha and Omega of Isaiah's ministry and mission.

This seven-fold sequence of biblical liturgy (Call→Praise→Confession→Forgiveness→Hearing God's Word→Responding to God's Word→Blessing) is the rhythm of worship that has shaped the faith of God's people for God's mission in the world. Such worship can help the church in our day to respond to God's call as Isaiah did, to say yes to God's call to work and witness in a world that still turns a deaf ear to God's Word.

Liturgy for a Lifetime

In fact, this liturgy is a godly rhythm for the whole of life, not just the worship of the church. What if this seven-fold rhythm were to mark our life and shape our faith every single day? What if, when we awake, we realize we've been called into wakefulness and enter into the praise of God for a new day? What if we confess that sin is crouching nearby and that our heart is "prone to wander," as the hymn says? What if, dependent on Jesus by the Spirit for forgiveness and wisdom, we hear God's Word as we read Scripture and respond to it throughout the day, like the man who built his house on a rock, with obedience and joy? And what if, when our head hits the pillow, we receive the blessing of God in our sleep (Ps. 127:2) until the new day begins? Such worship forms and reforms our faith for a lifetime.

Chapter 7

Living Mysteries:
Sacraments
and the
Education of
Christians

Fred P. Edie

Water splashes in the stone font at the front of the sanctuary, and a Christian is born. Nearby, a table is set, grace offered, simple bread and drink shared—and ordinary people find themselves reconciled, united in Christ's love, and witnesses to the grace they receive. These are the holy mysteries of God's self-giving. Sacramental worship offers nothing less than the invitation to meet God, to learn who God is, and to be transformed by this meeting. As such, it provides the church with a complete "curriculum" for Christian life. Congregations that are concerned for effective and faithful educational ministries will therefore treasure and encourage sacramental participation as a grace-filled means for forming persons to become Christian or more deeply Christian.

This chapter explores this sacramental "curriculum" (content to be taught) along with its "pedagogy" (how to teach that content). By "curriculum" I mean not merely a stack of shrink-wrapped leaflets for Sunday school but the whole Christian way of life: its knowledge, its practices, its virtues of character and affections of the heart. The first half of this chapter describes this sacramental curriculum and the way of life it entails; the second half deals with pedagogy, but there too I'm interested in more than "Ten Terrific Tips for Teaching." Borrowing from master Christian educator Charles Foster, I suggest instead three related pedagogical movements: (1) preparing for sacramental worship; (2) deep performance of and participation in sacramental worship; and (3) reflecting on sacramental worship in light of faithful Christian life. As we'll see, this third movement is necessarily connected to congregational ministries that extend beyond both sanctuary and classroom.

Sacramental Curriculum: Presence, Identity, Vocation

Sacraments may be described as a "curriculum" because there are at least three ways that they express or enact the Christian life.[1] First, worship through the sacraments teaches us where to look for and how to experience God's loving, grace-filled presence. Second, the sacraments teach us who this God is. By extension, sacramental revelation of God's identity provides worshipers with a deepened understanding of their own identity as God's people.

Third, sacramental worship bestows on the congregation their vocations ("callings") before God and for the world. In general, this vocation includes love of God and neighbor, but as we shall see below, sacramental worship further clarifies and concretizes Christian calling.

Sacraments and God's Presence

The church has always proclaimed that nurturing Christian faith requires people to actually meet the God who authors faith. Such a requirement implies, first of all, that Christians believe God is alive and well and available for meetings. These convictions are summed up nicely on a banner hanging outside a church near my home: "God is still speaking here." Consistent with the conviction that God continues to transform the world, sacraments are means to God's living, life-changing presence.

The Scriptures provide important clues to how this meeting occurs. For example, the apostle Paul provides his own perspective on God's presence in and through communion. While instructing the Corinthians on the holy meal, he reminds them of the formula passed down from Jesus, "Do this in remembrance of me" (1 Cor. 11:24-25). Biblical scholars point out that the Greek term *anamnesis*, usually rendered "remember" or "remembrance," is meant to convey more active force than the English terms signal. By relying on the English "remember" it becomes possible to view communion as merely a memorial of an event long past, with the living Jesus nowhere to be found: "We remember back in the day when Jesus shared the Last Supper with his disciples, but that was a really long time ago." But if we adjust the term slightly from *remember* to *re-member* it takes on an active, present tense power that is more faithful to the Greek. This shift is analogous to the shift from *represent* to *re-present*. In each case the hyphen nuances the meanings of the words to suggest that the past is not only recalled, it is *re-called* to present experience. We see therefore that, according to Paul's understanding, to participate in communion is to participate in *re-membering* God's mighty acts of the past—including especially the death and resurrection of Jesus Christ—into the present, with the expectation that the transformative power of these past events is also made present to worshipers today.

In related fashion, the writer of the Gospel of Luke signals that for his community engaging in the ritual meal means encountering the risen Christ, not just a mildewed memory (Luke 24:13-35).

The Scriptures hold a strong view of God's presence in and action through the sacraments. Put differently, sacraments are "means of grace," settings or practices where God's offer of loving relationship is especially and reliably present. God's people may trust that in their encounters with the baptismal waters and the communion meal, God shows up bearing gifts for their lives.

In addition to the offer of God's grace-filled presence to believers through the sacraments, we should note the manner of this presence in water, bread, and drink. These are ordinary, everyday things. God's presence through the ordinary is consistent with the doctrine of incarnation, the conviction that the mysterious God of the cosmos takes on the earthly human flesh of a particular human being—Jesus. So it is equally fitting that God chooses to reveal himself through earthly things like water and food or through ordinary human conventions like bathing and eating. Confidence in these modes of God's presence opens believers to encountering God in their everyday lives.

Sometimes Christians risk becoming atheists of the ordinary. They notice God at work only in the helicopter rescue of a child from a flash flood or in a miraculous recovery from cancer. No doubt God is capable of spectacular saves. But faith in God's presence through the sacraments helps Christians recognize how even ordinary, everyday life is animated by grace. Bathing an infant in the kitchen sink before bedtime or sitting down with family members to a dinner of leftovers, talking about nothing special after a long day of school and work—these too are sacramental sustenance for those with eyes to see, bodies to feel, and palates to taste.

Sacraments and God's Identity

Participating in the sacraments also educates believers into the identity of the God they meet there. We picked up some hints on God's identity in the previous section. This is a God who creates and blesses, who chooses to reveal himself through creation (most completely in the incarnation), and who is still working in creation through the power of the Holy Spirit toward the fullness of God's reign on earth. The sacraments identify God as triune. Another way to speak of God's identity is to suggest that God is "storied." Ultimately, God's story is salvation.

In brief, the story goes like this: God creates the world in love, including especially the two human beings. Tragically they rebel against God's loving provision, thinking they can do better on their own. This experiment ends poorly, and God opts for a rainy "do-over." God does not give up, but instead initiates a series of covenant agreements with God's people. God calls Abraham and Sarah and promises them land and countless descendents. God delivers the people from slavery in Egypt and into the Promised Land. In every case God is faithful to the covenant agreements but God's people are not. Ultimately, in a new and lasting covenant, God assumes responsibility both for God's own part of the bargain ("I will be your God") and the peoples' part ("We will be your people"). God does this by taking on humanity in Jesus Christ. In Christ, God restores the possibility of covenant fidelity. This possibility comes at great cost—the death of God's own Son—but in the resurrection God triumphs over death, putting an end to the seeming inevitability of human failure and the violence that accompanies it. The gift of the Holy Spirit births the church as witness to God's salvation and empowers its pilgrimage toward God's reign. This reign, begun already through Christ, will be fulfilled when he returns to rule in justice and peace. This is the story of who God is.

Each time Christians celebrate baptism or communion they tell this story—or better, they *enact* this story. One place to notice this telling is in either the prayer over the baptismal waters or the prayer of thanksgiving prior to sharing the communion bread and cup.

Take the baptismal prayers, for example. Not long after New Testament times, records emerge of prayers offered over the font prior to the water bath. Readers may find similar prayers in modern hymnals and worship books. These prayers lift up important events in God's story of salvation: creation by water, word, and Spirit; saving Noah, his family, and the animals through the flood; delivering God's people from slavery in Egypt through the waters of the Red Sea; crossing the Jordan River into the Promised Land; the prophetic cry for justice to flow like the waters; the birth of Jesus from his mother's womb, his baptism by John, his ministry of teaching and healing, including through water, his power to calm the seas, water flowing from his side at Golgotha, and meeting the disciples at the sea after his resurrection; the spread of the church across the Mediterranean Sea by baptism through water and the Spirit; the hope for God's reign fulfilled as imaged by the waters of the River of Life flowing to the heavenly city. Through this prayerful inspiration, the early church recognized how water, indeed how its baptismal waters, flowed through the past, to the present, and into the future of God's salvation story. To be baptized, therefore, is to be immersed in the story of God.

Sacraments and Practicing Vocation before God and for the World

Christians are called to love God and neighbor. But what does this vocation look like? Is it what I heard a teenager proclaim, "Smiling at people you don't like in the hallway at school"? Or is it "Just what God blesses me for because I'm good at it," as a wealthy businessman once suggested? Sacramental worship, because it is worship, invites us to one pole of Christian vocation (the work of glorifying and loving God through our worship), but we sometimes fail to recognize that it may also educate us into the more complicated work of loving our neighbors.

Recall that sacraments are means of grace. Sacraments convey the presence, power, and direction of the Holy Spirit upon believers, enabling them to turn away from their sinful lives. Baptism makes us "new creations" with callings to share in Christ's "ministry of reconciliation" (2 Cor. 5:17-19). Holy communion further specifies the shape of this reconciling ministry. For example, before gathering at the table Christians confess their sins and seek to be reconciled to God and neighbors. In addition, they pass Christ's peace throughout the assembly. Passing Christ's peace means way more than "Hi, how y'all doin'?"; it is instead a central gesture of restoring to loving relationship what our sin has fractured. In the breaking of bread and pouring out of drink, Christians *re-member* Christ's sacrifice at the hands of human violence as well as his rising again to overcome violence. To put it plainly, communion, through the gestures of confessing sin, passing peace, and receiving bread and cup, enacts worshipers into their reconciling vocations as peacemakers. How else are Christians to be known if not by their love?

Holy communion also invites Christians to cultivate their callings to receive and give hospitality. At communion the Host invites all people to his table. He feeds rich and poor alike, and this feeding contains the mystery of his very death and life. Fed, Christians are sent forth to feed hungry people and to create just systems for distributing food and the other necessities of life; to nourish the sick toward healing and create health care systems that include all persons; and to seek restoration for prisoners and others imprisoned by addiction or loneliness. Christians are fed by Christ so that they may become food for a world starving for reconciliation.

In summary, baptism and communion teach the possibility of God's loving presence to believers as well as the means of this presence. The sacraments rightly identify this God as One whose story involves the salvation of the world, and they both invite Christians to practice in worship and give clues for how they are to live out their ministry callings beyond the sanctuary—primarily as agents of Christ's ministry of reconciliation. The sacraments offer nothing less than a comprehensive educational curriculum for Christian faith and life.

Sacramental Pedagogy: Preparing for, Participating in, and Reflecting on Sacramental Life

How can we teach this sacramental curriculum? Following Charles Foster's proposal, we consider sacraments as central *events* in congregational life. We may devise pedagogies to help people both *prepare* for and then to *reflect* on the sacraments as means to deepened participation and heightened faithfulness.

Sacramental Worship as "Event-full"

For Foster, the power of congregational events to educate lies partly in their capacity to focus communal attention. By conjuring essential communal memories (as in the story of God's salvation) they may shape hopeful anticipation of the future. Congregational events display what God has done, what God is doing, and what God will do tomorrow. They also involve a particular congregation in God's action. All of this requires that an event be sufficiently "event-full," however.

That's why rich, excellent performance of sacramental worship is so important—performance that actively engages the bodies, minds, hearts, and souls of worshipers. In my own experience, sacraments often receive short shrift in the worship service. Pastors who are rock-solid when it comes to arranging for overflow parking on Easter Sunday morning may be clueless about presiding at the table in such a way as to invite worshipers to actually meet the risen Christ there. When sacraments are enacted in abbreviated, truncated, reductive, dismissive, blithe, crummy, and amateurish ways, worshipers quickly learn that they are meaningless. Performance can make or break sacramental Christian education.

By "performance" I am not suggesting that the actors in sacramental worship should strive to win Oscars, but rather that they strive to enact baptism and communion as richly as possible and with all the skill they can muster, so that the sacraments will be what they are intended to be. With respect to baptism, then, is there sufficient water for all involved to detect that this is, in fact, a bath and not merely a misting? Is the font suitably large and centrally located so that all worshipers may see the water, hear the water, and perhaps even be splashed by the water when children or adults are baptized? Are worshipers, especially children, invited to gather around those being baptized as a gesture of joyous covenantal support and to wonder at what God is doing in the sacrament? Are the prayers over the water and the baptized hearty and evocative, and do they involve the entire faith community? Do they tell God's story? Are members of the congregation commissioned for ministries of teaching, mission, and service in close proximity to the font as a sign of faithful response to the call to ministry that baptism entails?

With respect to communion, are the bread and cup set out on the table with sufficient style and grace so that worshipers readily discern that they are being invited to a meal? Do the bread and drink look, feel, and taste like what they are? Is grace offered before the community eats? Do the hosts/presiders model serenity, patience, hospitality? Does the sharing of the feast demonstrate the unity of Christ's body? Does the preached Word often gesture to the table? In all of this, do presiders model hope and joyous solemnity?

Excellent sacramental performance requires that worshipers, and especially worship leaders, be convicted that the sacraments are gifts from God and means of grace. It further requires that worshipers bring all their skill and imagination to practicing sacraments for what they are. Only through consistently excellent full-bodied performance will sacramental worship become sufficiently "event-full" as to be educative.

Preparation for Sacramental Worship

A second pedagogical key to education through sacramental worship is proper preparation. Some communities, following the pattern of the early church, schedule periods of education and formation in the years or seasons prior to a person's reception of the sacraments. Since baptism and communion are recurring events in congregational life, however, communities also may conceive of preparation as an ongoing process into deepened sacramental participation. Creative church educators will tailor and develop the following suggestions for their own settings.

Imaginative contemplation of symbols. Those responsible for educational leadership and planning should regularly invite people to give their ritual/symbolic/poetic ways of knowing a workout. This way of knowing is primarily associative, playful, evocative, and imaginative; it engages heart as readily as mind. Children do it naturally; adults need to be reminded how. Consider communal brainstorming on questions like these:

- What is the human significance of water?

- What encounters with water stand out in your own memory?

- What are some of the meanings of bread? Of wine (or grape juice)?

- What stories can you tell of food, feasting, and memorable meals? What "ingredients" combine to make meals memorable?

Questions like these invite worshipers to rediscover how everyday things and ordinary gestures that initially seem unremarkable evoke an extraordinary range of meanings and emotional valences. In other words, water and food, bathing and eating, all function symbolically in the imagination. Water means life, death, peace, terror; justice rolls down like the waters; the rain falls on the good and evil alike; water accommodates itself to what holds it; water destroys everything in its path, carving out grand canyons in the process. And this is only the surface of the mysteries of water. Any group will readily fill a chalkboard with responses to the question, "What is the human significance of water?"

An exercise like this intends to deepen our appraisal of the baptismal waters. By way of this imaginative work with the ritual symbol, we may better appreciate how biblical writers and leaders of the early church developed their theological understandings of baptism. Unsurprisingly, the baptismal waters also generate multiple theological meanings. They enact death to the old self; they are the womb through which the new creation is born; they are terrible and joyous; they mix difference into one Body; they generate power for holiness and justice; they transport the church toward God's reign. Note how the theological meanings are, like the meanings of water as a symbol, multiple, evocative, associative, and expansive. Exploring this range of meaning in symbols expands our capacities to meet and know God. In turn, deepened appreciation for ritual symbolic meaning opens our hearts to God's calling.

Connecting symbols to God's story of salvation. By way of exercises similar to those described above, worshipers may be invited to deepen their understanding of and participation in sacramental worship through a certain kind of biblical exploration. Beginning with the Old Testament, and then moving on to the New, church leaders could pose questions like these:

- What water-related stories can you recall from the Scriptures?

- What stories of food and feasting can you recall from the Scriptures?

My own experience suggests that even people who are not terribly biblically literate can be successful in these tasks when invited to have fun and work together. Sharing findings communally assures the fullest possible listings. Then ask questions like these:

- How do these stories combine to tell one grand story?

- How do the water-related stories contribute to your understanding of baptism?

- How do the stories of food and feasting contribute to the richness of communion?

In backdoor fashion, these questions invite people into the practice of allegorical (storied) readings of the Bible. Already evident in the writings of the Old and New Testaments, allegorical interpretation means viewing past events as prefiguring more recent ones. Following this line of interpretation, Noah's flood foreshadows Jesus' baptism by John; the sacrifice of the Passover lamb enabling Israel's liberation from slavery in Egypt prefigures Jesus' self-offering on the cross. Of course, allegory is not the only method for interpreting Scripture—used wrongly it can convey the impression that God's goings-on with Israel were just a warm-up act for Jesus. But as long as we are careful to acknowledge that Christianity does not cancel God's love for Israel, allegory can help deepen our engagement with the Scriptures and the sacraments. With respect to sacramental worship, it helps to connect the meanings of multiple biblical events with the meanings of the events of baptism and communion.

Theological interpretation of the sacraments. We have already seen how connecting diverse biblical stories to the sacraments becomes a means to interpret them theologically. In addition, explicit teaching and learning of sacramental theology is an important means to Christian education through the sacraments. In my own teaching I often use a list of theological categories dubbed by one of my former students as "Seven Theological Cs." The list includes Creation, Crisis, Covenant, Christ, Church, Calling, and the Coming Reign of God. After providing brief explanations of these terms as theological categories, I typically assign a number of biblical passages pertaining either to baptism or communion, and then invite people to explore what theological interpretations of the sacraments they find in them in light of this list. A selection of passages for baptism may include Matthew 3-4; John 3:1-7; Acts 2; Romans 6:3-11; 1 Corinthians 12:4-27; 2 Corinthians 5; 17-20; Galatians 3:26-29; 1 Peter 2:9-10; 3:18-22; Revelation 22:1-5. A selection of passages for communion may include Psalm 34:8; Luke 14:12-14; 22:1-23; 24:13-35; Acts 2:42-47; John 6; 1 Corinthians 5:6-8; 10:16-17; 11:17-29.

One case in point is Matthew's account of Jesus' baptism by John in the third chapter of his gospel. A theological interpretation of this text in light of baptism will note (as the church fathers did) that the three essential ingredients in this baptism—water, Spirit, Word from heaven—are the three ingredients also present at the dawn of creation (Gen. 1). It will also note that the Spirit descends in the form of a dove, thus linking baptism to Noah and the flood, to the renewal of creation, and to God's covenant love. It will detect the implicit naming of all three members of the Trinity. It will discover how in the words "This is my Son, whom I love; with him I am well pleased," Jesus' identity as Messiah, the suffering servant king is announced (see Ps. 2:7; Isa. 42:1). Finally, it will discern that as a result of his empowerment by the Spirit, Jesus takes up his ministry, declaring the advent of God's reign. In the brief span of one chapter, Matthew demonstrates how baptism is linked to the theology of creation or new creation, to covenant, to the nature of Jesus Christ, to Spirit empowerment, and to the calling to witness to God's reign. All this theology is embedded in baptism; a surplus of meaning in what some consider just "a little bath before brunch."

Reflecting on Sacramental Worship and Sacramental Life

As a third move in his pedagogical strategy, Foster encourages critical reflection on the events of congregational life. This kind of reflection invites individuals to create and/or name meaning out of their participation in the sacraments. Ideally these opportunities for reflection may be both personal and communal. For example, the person leading this reflection may ask an evocative question and invite people to journal privately. Group conversation is equally beneficial because it allows people to learn from each other's insights. Human beings are created to make self-conscious meaning out of their experiences, so the invitation to reflection encourages us toward greater clarity and ownership of the mystery of God's loving engagement with our lives through the sacraments.

Looking back and looking forward. As a general rule, reflection on sacramental participation should take its cue from the sacramental curricular content described above. Here are some questions that could be used:

- How is your participation in the sacraments an occasion to meet God in both familiar and surprising ways?

- What are you learning about God's identity, your own identity, and the identity of our community through the sacraments?

- What are you discerning of God's call to you or to our community through your participation in the sacraments?

Here are some reflection questions for the newly baptized or for parents and sponsors of the newly baptized:

- How did your time of preparation affect your participation in the sacrament of baptism?

- How did your experience of baptism confirm or confound your expectations?

- Where have you sensed God's presence and activity in the lead-up to baptism and in the actual sacrament? What have you learned about who God is and how God is calling you through this process?

- How does conceiving baptism as covenant help you to imagine it as shaping your future?

Here are some questions for recipients of holy communion:

- How has the range of meaning enacted in this simple feast shaped your participation in it?

- Which of the "Seven Theological Cs" have impacted your sense of what is going on in the meal and/or what God is doing in the world?

- How has participation in communion helped you to worship God, to understand God better, or to discern God's will for yourself or our church?

- Where have you found yourself thinking about communion in relation to your daily life?

- How has communion satisfied a hunger within you? Caused you to hunger more deeply?

Connecting the dots: sent forth to live sacramentally. Critically important to a pedagogy of Christian education in and through the sacraments is linking the sacraments to the congregation's other ministries of reconciliation. As we have seen, sacramental worship both *enacts* reconciling ministries and *empowers* people to take up their callings to share in Christ's ministries of justice, outreach, stewardship, hospitality, and healing beyond the sanctuary. Thus churches need to provide opportunities for the congregation to participate in such ministries so that imaginative and grace-filled links may be established.

Questions like these may be of help in connecting the dots between sacramental worship and engaging in reconciling ministries:

- How is this hurricane/flood relief mission we're on connected to our baptisms? (The watery implications of this particular mission are serendipitous but not required for this question to be useful.) How is God present/active in this work? How does this ministry teach us who God is? Who we are?

- How does our baptismal covenant cause us to think about water stewardship on our church grounds and at home?

- Whose feet need washing in our neighborhood?

- How is our after-school program for children an ark of salvation?

- How is our monthly meal with folks at the shelter inspired by communion? Where is God in this? How has it affected your ongoing reception of the sacrament in worship?

- How does Christ's simple feast with the church invite us to consider the goodness of living more simply?

- What is the relationship between the bread and wine/juice of the Lord's Supper and our consumption of fast food?

* * *

Sacramental worship matters fundamentally to educating for faithful Christian life. It teaches people how to engage with the mystery of God's presence, how to know who this God is, and what to do with their own lives as a result. Wise educators understand that these educational implications of the sacraments are simply too important to neglect. They will seek to heighten the sacraments' formative impact on believers by preparing them to participate in the sacraments, by assuring that sacramental worship is rich and full, and by calling the congregation to take up ministries that imaginatively incarnate the sacraments in daily life. In this way Christians are educated in their faith while God's grace is extended into the world.

For Further Reading

- Laurence Hull Stookey's *Baptism: Christ's Act in the Church,* and *Eucharist: Christ's Feast with the Church* will deepen readers' understanding of and appreciation for the sacraments.

- Jerome Berryman's *Godly Play* and my own *Book, Bath, Table, and Time* describe in more detail educational approaches that assume the centrality of Christian worship.

- Charles Foster's *Educating Congregations* describes his approach to "eventful" Christian education.

- *Sourcebooks* on Baptism and Eucharist from Liturgy Training Publications excerpt passages from the Christian tradition, important thinkers past and present, and great literature, to encourage deepened imagination into sacramental mystery.

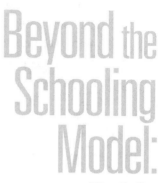

Chapter 8

Beyond the Schooling Model:
Faith Formation in the Educational Context

Marian R. Plant

We called the series "Candles on the Table for Life." It was offered over a six-week period on Sunday mornings for adult education. I had offered to plan and lead each session. The idea was to focus on one biblical narrative each week—either read directly from the biblical text or told freestyle—to recount a personal connection with the narrative, and to invite others to make connections with the narrative. The goal was to voice Scripture's power to sustain and guide us, and to make participants aware of that power, even if that awareness came in retrospect.

One week the session was titled "Deadly Waiting." I recounted the narratives of Jesus' crucifixion and resurrection, including the period of desolation until Jesus' followers realized that their rabbi and redeemer was alive. I told them of my difficulty in remembering the exact date of my father's death—a confession that shocked several people and puzzled others until I went on to explain that my dad died on Holy Saturday. So it is mid-morning of Holy Saturday each year, regardless of the date, that is the anniversary of my father's death for me.

Then I told them of a time in my professional life when I had had to do something absolutely terrifying. I needed to participate in a confrontation with another clergy person, one who had considerably more power and authority than me. I was informed on a Friday morning that the meeting would take place the coming Monday evening. By Friday afternoon the anxiety was almost paralyzing.

I called a trusted clergy friend who had experience and great wisdom in such matters. I told her what was happening. I told her I believed in the resurrection and in a resurrection faith. I told her I knew there would be life for me again after all this, but right now it was nothing but Good Friday. She listened carefully. She said that we Christians know Good Friday—and we recognize Good Fridays in our own lives. We also know that Easter means resurrection, and that it comes on the third day. We've had our own Easter experiences as well. What we aren't so aware of is the time between the end of Good Friday and the dawn of Easter morning, the time of limbo with the entrance to the tomb sealed and all our worst fears for company. "You are in that limbo now," she said. "It's awful. And all we can do is hold on until our Easter comes." My friend named what I was experiencing within the framework of our common faith story. She called it the "Deadly Waiting."

I told the adults gathered that Sunday morning that naming what I was experiencing did not make that time any less awful for me. Yet something shifted, reorienting me, recentering me, grounding me at a third soul-point instead of just two: Good Friday . . . Deadly Waiting . . . Easter.

When I finished telling my story, I looked around the circle of faces and gently asked, "When have you found yourself in 'deadly waiting'? Would you be willing to share with us?" And for the next forty minutes we listened to one another make faith-sense of experiences that until now had not had a faith name. I watched the changing expressions on participants' faces as this occurred: first thoughtful, as they searched their experiences; then tentative, as they gave voice to situations they'd identified; and then a sort of "oh" as faith and experience introduced themselves to one another and smiled.

* * *

I share this experience because it illustrates both the challenge and the potential for authentic faith formational experiences within the context of the local church. The challenge lies in examining the limits of educational ministries as they've developed over recent decades. The potential lies in moving beyond those limitations.

For at least the past fifty years, educational ministries have generally followed a "schooling" model. Specific times are designated for education, often explicitly called Sunday school or church education, in contrast to fellowship time and worship time. *Classes* are organized by age level; typically with few opportunities for multigenerational engagement within the faith community. *Classrooms* are created and designed for church school use, and *curriculum* is written and organized to take advantage of teaching methods used in grade schools: word games, coloring sheets, fill-in-the-blanks, crafts, and art projects. It tends to be text-heavy, with few, if any, pictures or maps. Youth are expected to learn the information from their teachers. Curriculum for adults is similarly text-heavy. Teachers of adult classes are expected to either prepare a lesson from the book or lead a discussion that moves the class through the material to the desired knowledge by the end of class. Regardless of its target age levels, most curricula is geared for imparting content—be it Bible verses and stories, creeds and doctrines, or positions of the church on social issues. And teachers of all ages are regarded as authorities, whether by virtue of being the pastor, seniority in the congregation, or simply because of the title.

But Christian educators have come to realize three things: first, the "school" model used by the church for its educational ministries has lasted at least three decades too long; second, the idea that "content equals information to learn" has morphed into "content" being isolated from faith practice and discipleship; and third, the focus on "content equals information to learn" has been far too narrow to foster and sustain a lifetime of faith formation. The necessity before us is to widen the focus of our ministries within the educational context of the local church and to adopt approaches that are more conducive to faith formation.

Let's look, for example, at teaching the beliefs of the church: the confessional statements, doctrines, and creeds that form the core of our identity as individual believers and as the church. In the "content equals information to learn" model, people are introduced to the belief statements, instructed in their meaning, told the importance to our salvation of adhering to them, and set to the task of committing them to heart—the assumption being that this kind of instruction will lead to faith formation. That is to say, they will feel invited "into relationship with God, self, others, and creation"; they will have come to know themselves as Christians, "having assimilated the values, beliefs, and lifestyle of one who professes to be a follower of Jesus Christ"; they will respond to knowledge of God's grace by taking up the life of discipleship, "the discipleship of loving God and all God's creation, including our neighbors."[1]

If only that were so! But the dropout rate after people make profession of faith or confirmation remains discouragingly high across most local congregations, and the absence of parents who encourage their children to participate in church school, worship, and mission/outreach projects speaks volumes about the failure of the "content equals information to learn" model to nurture and sustain authentic faith formation in the generations of the 1980s, 1990s, and 2000s.

So how might we widen the focus of teaching the beliefs of the church beyond "content equals information to learn" in order to foster and sustain faith formation not only among children, youth, and new believers, but also among confessing adults? One possibility is to teach beliefs and confessional statements in the presence of conversations and actions that demonstrate the power of those beliefs in people's everyday lives. For example, each belief/faith statement below could be followed up with a "How?" invitation. Here are a few possibilities.

Belief/Faith Statement	"How?" Invitation	"Experience" Statements
I believe in God.	How do you feel God with you? What's that like for you?	I feel God with me when . . .
I believe in Jesus Christ.	How is the way you work at your job different because of your awareness of Jesus' presence?	I'm aware of Jesus Christ as a living presence as I . . .

The "experience" statements come from members of the group as they think through the belief statements together. They are not "experts," except in their willingness to think out loud and to share experiences that were faith formational.

The beauty of widening the focus of our educational ministries beyond "content equals information to learn" is that it dissolves the rigid divisions between age levels. In the scenario above, for instance, a young person may be invited to give his or her testimony to new believers in the course of their adult discipleship instruction. Meanwhile, in children's church school, catechism, or confirmation classes, conversations exploring what the church's beliefs look and feel like in the lives of peers and adults bring the beliefs to life.

From "Content Equals Information to Learn" to "Faith in Formation"

I love Legos. Big fat chunky ones and little specialized ones. The thing about Legos is that they're concrete but limited only by imagination. I tell my Christian education and pre-seminary students that a kit with some markers, masking tape, blank paper, pens or pencils, and Legos equips them for education in just about any place, time, or subject. I've used Legos at the first meeting of a Christian education board after the new members have been elected. One year I told the group that in a few minutes, they'd be asked to respond to the question "Why were you willing to say yes to serving on this board?" Then I dumped a sizeable pile of Legos onto the coffee table and asked everyone to use them to symbolize their vision for the educational ministries of the church. The vision could be for just this year or for the long term.

Some dove into the activity with gusto, others with trepidation— "I'm no good at stuff like this." But no one stayed in their comfy parlor chairs. They had to move to reach the Legos, and many found the floor to be a great place to stay. From there they could reach everything they needed, and they could swap with others for pieces they wanted.

The task became play, and the outcome was remarkable. When I called time on the construction activity and the group began sharing why they'd said yes to serving on the Christian education board and explaining their vision for their church's educational ministries, it was clear that they had looked further inside themselves and thought more deeply about their faith than was usual, at least in regard to serving on a board or committee. One person said, "I didn't think about either of your questions when I said yes to the nominating committee; I just figured it was my turn to serve on a church board. But now I realize that deep down I'm willing to serve because it matters what we do for our kids and teens and adults as they grapple with faith stuff." Someone else said, "I'm not really sure what I have to contribute, but [Shirley] thought I'd be good. Now I'm determined not to let her down, or the faith she has in me. With God's help, I won't."

Then there were the constructions themselves. One man built an intricate structure that had branches leading out of part of it. He explained that his vision was to build on whatever was solid already—to use what was working as our foundation—but also explore people's needs and create whatever new ministries were necessary to support them in their faith and personal growth.

A woman held up a Lego door frame complete with a door that opened and closed. She said, "I'm really no good at building things, but I found this door lying among all the Legos, and for me it represents that Christian education flows both ways. In my vision, we are always opening the door to faith experiences and learning about the Bible, our traditions, our denomination, and our responsibilities as Christians. But we're also willing to step outside of this church building and our ways of doing things in order to discover how God is working in people's lives, no matter what age they are."

Then the superintendent held up her creation and announced, "This is a wagon that's *loaded* with everything that has to be done this year in order for the church school to be successful. See the handle? That handle doesn't just have my name on it. My vision is for lots of people—not just those with children in church school right now— to grab that handle and help us get to where we need to go this year. Oh, and notice there's lots of room around the sides for people to help push! This is a *huge* ministry, and it belongs to everyone." In what would normally have been a dry, almost intimidating first-of-the-year meeting, laughter and good humor reigned. So did the dynamics of faith formation.

As exciting as the Legos-meet-the-Christian education board meeting was, using Legos with a confirmation class was even better. We'd come to the place in the program where we focus on the vows young people take during the confirmation. For the next several weeks, the topic ("content") would be personal faith and discipleship. These eighth graders had all grown up playing with Legos. Their eyes lit up when I poured the blocks onto the table. We chatted about who had what Lego sets, which were their favorites, and who still had Lego projects at home. Then I turned them loose with the instruction to create a symbol of their faith using the Legos.

Fifteen very quiet, very focused minutes later, everyone was finished. I asked them to show their creations and to explain the symbolism. What those young people articulated was rich and deep and moving. They included stories of loss and grief—the death of grandparents, siblings, a mother; separation and divorce of parents; moves to new towns; stepfamilies. They included celebrations and accomplishments—in school, Scouts, or sports. They included doubts and convictions, the presence of God in remarkable and ordinary circumstances, and the feeling of safety and acceptance they experienced only at church.

Had I simply started the session that session with, "What does faith mean to you" or "How would you describe your Christian faith," I'm convinced that an excruciatingly long silence, broken only with reluctant and tentative answers, would have followed. Look what occurred instead. These eighth graders and their pastor shared in each other's experience of relationship with God, themselves, others, and creation. Together we discovered that each had come to know her- or himself as a Christian; each had already assimilated many of the values and beliefs of those who profess themselves to be followers of Jesus Christ. These young people stood at the shoreline, so to speak, wading into and out of the waters of faith expression with one another. They witnessed each other responding to the knowledge of God's grace in their lives, moving that much closer to taking up lives of discipleship. That evening there was no such thing as "content in isolation." That evening, faith in formation filled each breath we took.

From Content in Isolation to Faith in Formation

Here's an exercise in applying the principles we've been talking about. Look at the three situations we've covered: "Deadly waiting," "Legos meet Christian education board," and "Confirmation class Legos" and then respond to the following:

- Identify elements in common across all three narratives. Be sure to write down what you identify so you can refer to that list as you go along.

- Using the list of common elements just identified, consider the following:

   o Which elements fit the "content equals information to learn" (schooling) model discussed earlier in the chapter? In what way? Write down your insights.

   o Which elements do not fit that model? In what way(s)? Write down your insights.

- What transformed the three educational ministry settings from "content in isolation" to occasions for "faith in formation"? Be as specific as you can as you write down your ideas.

Now consider your own faith community setting.

- Where in your educational ministries context is "content in isolation" still present? Make a list. Be specific; think about all age levels and settings.

- Pick out one particular ministry. Brainstorm the steps that could transform it into a more intentional "faith in formation" context. List the steps you brainstorm.

- Review your ideas; then create a possible step-by-step approach to transforming that ministry as brainstormed above. Write out the plan. Share it with an appropriate leader within your faith community setting.

Practice Field and Postgame Review

Faith-full, real-life living is essential to faith formation. It is the partner of "faith in formation" educational contexts. Fortunately, the educational settings of local churches can function as the practice fields, helping us prepare for our faith-full living beyond the church's walls. Consider the following faith-full practices:

- giving to others

- caring for others

- steeping oneself in Scripture

- planning and practicing a prayer life

- championing the oppressed

It has been my experience that churches fare pretty well at encouraging these practices in their members as long as they provide institutional support for ministries or programs where members can "plug in": offerings for missions or families with special needs; disaster relief; homebound visits; food pantries or hot meal programs; "adopt-a-family" opportunities; Bible study groups; worship leadership opportunities; devotions at the beginning of committee and board meetings; prayer circles; parenting sessions; working with people who are homeless; offering fair trade gift items for purchase; mission trips for youth and adults; and more.

The breakdown in faith formation practice comes once people step outside the church doors and the practice fields the church provides for them. That's because church leaders often assume that members of the congregation will automatically generalize their faith practices within the programmatic and architectural structure of the church into their daily lives, 24/7. In the vast majority of instances, this isn't the case.

One way to bridge this "disconnect" between our practice field (the church) and our daily life is to create what I'll call the "postgame review." Postgame review, a staple of sports teams, needs to be a staple of the church's educational contexts as well. This is not a gripe session or a program evaluation session, though program review has its own value. In postgame review, members of the congregation share their individual insights, quandaries, and failings with one another *so as to better equip themselves to live faith-filled lives daily.* This kind of review is characterized by "I" statements and questions:

- I found a way to free up some time by . . . By doing this I can now . . .

- I feel like I'm just not being helpful at my job. What else can I try?

- I keep forgetting to practice what I decided I'd do. What's working for you that I might try?

- I'm having a tougher time than I thought changing my spending habits. I want to give more to others, but I keep thinking "I really want that sweater; it goes great with the slacks I already have." And then I start feeling like I'll be deprived if I give the money to someone else. I could use some help making the switch to faithful, less selfish living.

Intentionality is key to incorporating postgame review into the life and programs of our congregations. From first-hand experience in a group of twenty church lay leaders, I can tell you that about a third will embrace such postgame review, a third will try it out and be lukewarm, and the rest will be agitated by having to participate, though they might not say so openly at first. On the other hand, congregants as a whole may respond far more enthusiastically to the opportunity to move forward in integrating their faith and their daily life in the company of others who are trying to do the same. So be brave. Figure out creative ways to host postgame reviews in conjunction with the faith formational/educational ministry "practice fields" your church already has in place. Work on this for all ages in age-appropriate ways. Bring food. Sit in a comfortable space. Light a candle on a table in your midst and invite God's Holy Spirit into your review. Begin the conversation with your own "I statement" about something you're working on or trying to bring more fully into your life. Invite others to do the same. Eat and talk together, keeping faith-full living at the center, and always bringing your humanity as a child of God into the circle. You will be amazed.

Transforming the Schooling Model to Sacred Space and God's Playground

Most of us look for step-by-step instructions and how-to manuals when we want to fix or simply improve things that need work. I invite you to adopt a slightly different approach. Realize that you will be "making the road by walking it."[2] Even as you adapt the insights and examples I have provided in this chapter to your own setting, keep in mind that you will learn as much, if not more, from your experiences together. Experiment, tinker with your experiments, and experiment again. Push yourself to try some things that haven't been done before. Remember that it's less about program and all about deeper faith formation and experience. When you wonder if you've wandered into some wilderness, use the following exercise to help reorient yourself.

- When is faith most real to me? When do I experience my faith most consciously?

- What might we do better together as a multiage community than in separate classes?

- What is available to us in our setting and with our people that could move our education ministries from "content equals information to learn" to faith in formation?

May God's blessings be with you in all your faith-formational endeavors.

Chapter 9

No Better Place:

Fostering Intergen- erational Christian Community

Holly Catterton Allen

The icebreaker question in our small group was "What are you afraid of?" Here are some of the responses:

- spiders (Jennifer, a teen)

- gaining too much weight in my pregnancy (Amy, twenty-something)

- that I will die young like my dad did (Kevin, forty-something)

- that I won't pass fourth grade (Nolan, a fourth grader)

- that I won't be able to finish my thesis (Chris, a graduate student)

- that my cancer will return (Carlos, sixty-something)

- that Ben won't get parole (Jan, thirty-something)

Then it was Jeremy's turn. He was a second grader at the time. He put his head on his arm and began to cry. In a small, jerking voice, he said, "I'm afraid to go to sleep because I have nightmares." One of the dads in the group immediately came over to Jeremy and put his arm around his shoulders. He held him for a minute, then prayed with him and over him. Then one of the older elementary girls in the group came over and said, "You know, Jeremy, I sometimes have nightmares—I know how you feel. I always pray and then I feel better." With awe in her voice, a young adult, a new Christian in the group said, "I was reading the Psalms this morning and I found a Scripture for you—Psalm 4:8, 'I go to bed and sleep in peace. Lord, you keep me safe.'"

Although this type of intergenerational ministry is common in our small groups, it is rare in contemporary American Christianity—for the simple and obvious reason that the generations rarely gather together to allow for intergenerational ministry to occur.

Over the past hundred years our society has increasingly separated families and segregated age groups. Age-graded public education, the movement from extended to nuclear families, and the prevalence of retirement and nursing homes for older persons and preschools for the young have all contributed to a general segregation of young and old.

In the past, churches were among the few places where families, singles, couples, children, teens, grandparents—all generations—came together on a regular basis. Yet the societal trend toward age segregation has also moved into the church. Age-based classes for children as well as adults, programming for teens, and various worship options tend to separate families and age groups from each other. As a result, children and adults may go through their whole lives experiencing the gathering of Christians as an age-segregated phenomenon.

Fortunately, some people are beginning to question this late twentieth-century development. A recent issue of *Leadership Journal* (Summer 2009) asked the question, "Is the era of age segregation over?" and the publication of at least three recent books promoting a more intergenerational Christian culture indicate that indeed the time has come to question this late twentieth-century phenomenon.[1]

In this chapter we'll explore three interrelated questions:

- Why, in recent decades, have churches tended to separate the generations?

- What are the spiritual benefits of bringing the generations back together?

- What kinds of intergenerational structures can churches introduce to encourage optimum spiritual growth for everyone?

Why Do Churches Separate the Generations?

Several factors have contributed to the age segregation so many Christians experience when they gather for worship, service, ministry, or simply for fellowship. The previously mentioned societal move toward age segregation in general is one factor; generational preferences, changing music styles, and church growth recommendations are other causes. One last factor is that since the mid-twentieth century, church leaders have recognized the importance of developmental issues.

Developmental theory indicates that people go through various developmental stages from birth through adulthood. Jean Piaget's cognitive theory, Erik Erikson's psychosocial theory, James Fowler's faith development theory, and Daniel Levinson's life stage theory have all contributed to the understanding that persons of different ages are at different stages of development, and that they tend to work, learn, and grow best in settings that focus on the needs of that age and/or stage.

For example, Piaget's work in cognitive development revolutionized preschool and elementary public education in the 1960s and 1970s, and later did the same for Sunday schools in the 1980s and 1990s. Educators implemented age-appropriate teaching and learning practices for children—using all five senses and encouraging body movement, visual aids, and active involvement. These are all excellent ideas. Eventually developmental concerns were applied not only to Sunday school, but to the worship hour, youth groups, and other church-related activities. Erikson's psychosocial theory (as well as other developmental theories) indicates that persons from ages thirteen to twenty have unique needs, such as identity and autonomy issues, that other age groups may not have. Levinson's and others' life stage theories note that while young adults are building careers and parenting young children, middle adults are parenting teens and caring for their own aging parents, and older adults may be dealing with serious illness, loss of income, and relocation to residential care facilities.

In other words, the different ages and stages of life are very dissimilar, yielding groups of people with widely differing needs and expectations. It follows, then—or so church leaders have reasoned—that persons in each of these developmental stages need special stage-related programs. Of course, developmental theorists make a valid point—children and adults *do* learn differently, and

teenagers and senior citizens do have quite different life-stage needs.
So what is the problem?

The fundamental difficulty is that *spiritual* development is not essentially *cognitive* or *psychosocial* development. Spiritual development is not connected solely to one's stage in life. Other factors—not all primarily age-specific—are at work in spiritual development. Therefore applying age-related developmental principles to a primarily spiritual enterprise could be problematic, even detrimental.

This does not mean that it's necessary for the generations to be together all of the time—there can and should be frequent opportunities for young adults, teens, children, and older adults to address specific age- or stage-related issues that impact their spiritual lives. But it is the premise of this chapter that the ways people of all ages are alike are more important than the ways in which they are different, and that bringing the generations together creates opportunities for unique spiritual benefits for all.

How Can Intergenerational Settings Contribute to Spiritual Growth?

This section will look at the reasons for developing an intentional intergenerational church culture. It will explore biblical, theoretical, and empirical rationale for the idea that intergenerational faith communities offer unique opportunities for everyone to grow spiritually.

Biblical Support for Intergenerational Community

In Scripture, coming to know God is typically presented as a family- and community-based process. God's directives for his people in the Old Testament clearly identify the Israelites as a relational community in which children were to participate in the culture they were part of. Children were not just included; they were drawn in, assimilated, and absorbed into the whole community with a deep sense of belonging. The directives for religious feasts and celebrations illustrate this point best. These festivals, including Passover, the Feast of Weeks, the Feast of Booths, and the Feast of Trumpets,[2] included elaborate meals, dancing, music, singing, and sacrifices. All of Israel—from the youngest to the oldest—participated. As children and teens sang, ate, listened to stories, and asked questions, they came to know who they were, who God was, and what God had done for his people in ages past.

Emerging from its Jewish heritage, the early church was a multigenerational entity. All generations met together, worshiping, breaking bread, praying together, and ministering to one another in the context of the home (Acts 2:46-47; 4:32-35; 16:31-34). Besides meeting with parents and others in house churches, children were clearly present in other spiritual settings as well. In Acts 16:15, Lydia was baptized with "the members of her household"; in Acts 16:33, the jailer "and all his household" were baptized. Also in Acts we read the story of the young man, Eutychus, who fell out of a window while listening to Paul preach until midnight (Acts 20:7-12). And Luke reports that children accompanied those bidding farewell to Paul as he boarded a ship at Tyre (Acts 21:5-6).

These Scripture passages indicate that intergenerational community was apparently the norm for Jewish and Christian gatherings in the first century. Recognizing this intergenerational emphasis throughout Scripture prompts us to ask, "Have educational psychologists or pedagogical theorists explored the learning principles that might explain the importance of such an emphasis?"

A Learning Theory for Cultivating Intergenerational Faith

Intergenerational Christian experience (IGCE) has been a practice in search of a theory. At this point, those who extol the benefits of IGCE[3] ground their (extra-biblical) theory in the work of social scientists such as G. H. Mead, Margaret Mead, and Erik Erikson; developmentalists such as Jean Piaget and James Fowler; and religious educationists such as John Westerhoff III, Donald Miller, Ellis Nelson, and James Michael Lee. Yet no broad learning theory for IGCE has been proposed.

Sociocultural Learning Theory, or the "Potty Training Phenomenon"
Potty training our first son, David, was an interminable process. After purchasing a popular book on the subject, creating a chart for stickers, and gathering small treats as rewards, we began the arduous process. Months later we were still slogging through. When it came time to train our second son, Daniel, I reluctantly dug out the book, bleakly sought courage to tackle the task, and generally dreaded the ordeal. One day as I walked into the laundry room/bathroom with a load of clothes, I came upon our older son demonstrating to a very intent younger brother the basic technique of aiming straight; David had pulled up a small stool for his little brother to stand on, and Daniel was well on his way to proficiency. I was delighted! This potty training phenomenon—that the firstborn child is the most difficult to potty train, and the next child learns from the first and so on—illustrates well the learning theory that follows.

In my dissertation[4] I proposed the situative/sociocultural perspective as introduced by Lev Vygotsky[5] and developed and elaborated by contemporary educational psychologists and social scientists to explain the basic learning principles at work in an intergenerational Christian community. A key concept for understanding Vygotsky's sociocultural theory is the zone of proximal development (ZPD). The concept of ZPD is the idea that when a person is ready to learn the next thing, the best way to learn it is to be with those who are just ahead on the learning journey. This concept is not a new one, though perhaps it has not been well articulated in educational terms. As I mentioned earlier, mothers of several children know ZPD as the "potty-training phenomenon."

Vygotsky would say that people learn to be members of their community as they actively participate in that particular community, learning alongside those who are further ahead in the journey. Intergenerational Christian settings are authentic, complex learning environments, made up of individuals at various stages in their faith journeys who are teaching some people and learning from others as they participate in their community of believers.

Situated Learning—Becoming a Midwife

In order for my friend Allison to become a midwife, she spent a year as an apprentice with an experienced midwife attending dozens of home and hospital births. Though she was already a registered nurse with the required college degree, Allison has told me that the year of apprenticeship is what made her a midwife.

Another way of explaining the unique benefits of an intergenerational faith culture is to examine the idea of "situated learning," the kind of learning that happens in apprenticeships. Researchers Lave and Wenger coined the phrase *situative learning* as they examined studies of several apprenticeship settings, including midwives, tailors, and meat cutters. In situated activity, individuals must be given access to the practices they are expected to learn and to participate in the activities and concerns of the group, such as Allison attending and participating in the birthing of babies. At first, learners are relatively peripheral in the activities of a community, but as they become more experienced and adept, their participation becomes more central. This participation must be legitimate—in other words, they must actually practice the activities themselves, not just observe or receive instruction about them. Eventually Allison coached a mother through childbirth with the master midwife watching quietly from the corner of the room.

Situative learning approaches fit what those who promote inter-generational Christian approaches have been saying for years—to be a Christian one must participate fully in Christian community. If novice midwives and tailors learn best by participating fully with practicing midwives and tailors, then perhaps Christians learn best from participating fully with practicing Christians further along on the journey. Intergenerational faith cultures provide continual opportunities for this type of learning to take place.

Support from Research Studies

For my field research on the spirituality of children, I interviewed forty children, ages nine to eleven, who were regular attendees in six churches. Half of the children participated in an intergenerational small group and worshiped with their parents in an intergenerational worship setting. The other half of the children attended Sunday school, children's church, and some type of other midweek gathering, but they did not participate in any intergenerational setting.

The results of my research revealed several spiritual differences between those who participated regularly in intergenerational settings and those who did not. The most significant difference was in the area of prayer. Children in the intergenerational (IG) group referred to prayer significantly more times in their interviews than did the children from non-IG settings. With respect to the concept of knowing God, more IG children in this sample gave relational descriptions of that concept than did non-IG children. Although both groups of children gave profound and eloquent testimony to their relationship with God, the IG children in this sample were more *aware* of their relationship with God; that is, they spoke more often and more reciprocally of that relationship than did children in the other group.

Kara Powell of the Fuller Youth Institute at Fuller Theological Seminary is currently in the middle of a three-year College Transition Project looking at the faith journeys of four hundred youth group graduates. Though the study is not complete, it already reveals that youth who participate in "intergenerational relationships in church are showing promise for stronger faith in high school and beyond."[6]

Both Peter Marr[7] and James White[8] report positive results from their studies of intergenerational settings. They report that participants seem to enjoy intergenerational opportunities; after they experience them, they seem to like being in age-inclusive settings; they like interrelating with each other; intergenerational friendships develop; intergenerational ministry occurs more frequently. In other words, intergenerational events seem "to draw the people of a church closer together."[9]

Kathleen Chesto administered a survey to participants in an intergenerational faith program who met for a year. Chesto's research found that they talked about God and read the Bible more after participating in the program. The participants offered numerous strengths of the program: "It helps families to pray together, to share with other people, to be more open, to grow," and "The children become more comfortable expressing their feelings about God and they see their parents doing so."[10]

The anecdotal and empirical support that exists offers enticing and promising benefits for regular cross-generational gatherings of the body of Christ. And church leaders are beginning to ask what these intergenerational settings would look like and how churches can transition to a more age-integrated culture in which people of all ages can grow in their faith together.

What Kinds of Intergenerational Structures Offer Optimum Spiritual Growth?

Most churches already offer occasional intergenerational activities such as dinners and "fellowship time," church-wide service projects, or annual musicals or cantatas in which children and adults participate together. While these are excellent means of providing intergenerational experiences, the ultimate goal is for churches to become intergenerational in their outlook and practice. This will not happen simply by adding an occasional intergenerational activity. It will require a paradigm shift guided by leaders who understand the issues and communicate well. Here are some suggestions for church leaders who desire to cultivate a more intergenerational approach for worship, Bible study, and ministry:

- Revisit the basic goals or purposes of Christian education/spiritual formation, which may be expressed in terms of commitment to Christ, growing in Christ, or Christian maturity. The usual questions that follow such a discussion are, "How well are we meeting our goal?" and "What else can we do?" In this case, the question is, "How can an intergenerational approach foster our goal?"

- Contrast/compare the spiritual needs of older adults, middle adults, young adults, single adults, teens, and children, ultimately recognizing the surprising similarities.

- Discuss the factors that have led churches to develop age-segregated approaches to church and religious education (such as developmental concerns and societal norms).

- Study the biblical examples of Jewish community life and early house churches, perhaps exploring the relational dynamics of such settings.

- Share the theoretical support (for example, from this chapter) for learning socioculturally and intergenerationally.[11]

- When it is deemed feasible, begin taking steps to reintegrate the generations.

This last step would need to be a multistage undertaking, beginning at a simple, less disruptive level and moving to more complex levels later as the church begins to recognize the blessing and benefits for people of all ages.

Intergenerational activities in Christian settings can take a variety of forms. Several promising possibilities are described below.

Including children in worship. If children or teens are normally separated during the primary worship service, search for ways to include the children for fifteen to twenty minutes (or more) of praise in the Sunday morning worship on a regular basis (once a month, every fifth Sunday, every other week, or *all the time*). Major religious educationists (Westerhoff, Fowler)[12] recommend this approach, as do intergenerational advocates (Gambone, Glassford, Prest, Rendle, White).[13] Simply stated, children need to be participating with the significant adults in their life, worshiping, praying, and listening to God's Word.

Special programs. Another common intergenerational activity is including children in special events like celebrations for graduating seniors of the church or retiring ministers.

Intergenerational events. Some churches may wish to use an intergenerational group to plan one or more events a year: a Thanksgiving program, a short drama for Easter, a Christmas musical, or some other event that requires time, effort, creativity, brainstorming, and work for a group of people of all ages.

Bible study. This approach might take a variety of forms—for example, an intergenerational Sunday school class, a whole congregational study, or intergenerational small groups. A few churches have experimented with intergenerational Sunday school classes, typically focusing on such topics as the fruit of the Spirit or the Beatitudes. Here are some suggestions for churches that wish to establish a successful intergenerational Sunday school program:

- o offer it as an option

- o determine an age limit (such as seven years and up)

- o limit the study to six to ten weeks

- o recruit the most creative and experienced adult, youth, and children's teachers to collaborate in constructing the teaching/ learning materials

At the full congregational level, the church as a whole could focus on a particular biblical concept for worship and teaching. For example, the whole church could study several names of God and incorporate those into worship. Adults and children who have experienced God as Yahweh Jireh (the LORD our provider) or El Roi (the God who sees) could share their testimonies with everyone together. Intergenerational groups could create banners that depict each name. Sermons could focus on these names. And at the end of the series, an intergenerational group could present a drama illustrating the names.

Service. Rebuilding after hurricanes, serving food in soup kitchens, participating in mission trips, and other forms of service lend themselves to intergenerational involvement. Whenever any group—preschoolers, teens, young adults, older adults—decides to serve, give, and share, encourage them to ask, "How can we include another generation in our efforts?"

Intergenerational small groups. A more comprehensive (even radical) approach would be forming weekly (or biweekly) intergenerational small groups for ministry, fellowship, prayer, worship, and/or Bible study. Because it is so radical, churches may be fearful of such an approach until they begin to see some of the potential benefits.

For four years our family worshiped with a church that promoted intergenerational small groups every Sunday evening. These groups changed my understanding of children and of spiritual formation. As a result of these new understandings, I changed my career. Forming intergenerational small groups is the most important recommendation I will make in this chapter—but it is the hardest to implement. Here's what those groups looked like:

Icebreakers. The opening vignette of this chapter illustrates the kind of intergenerational ministry that can and does happen—even, at times, during the icebreaker. Usually, the icebreaker is light and fun—a question such as "What did you enjoy most at the Fourth of July fireworks celebration?" But no matter what the question, the format for the answer is always the same. Each adult and each teen, each college student and each child responds by saying, for example, "My name is Enrico, and we lit firecrackers at our friend's house out by the lake." That way we all get to know each others' names and some of the pieces in our lives that make each of us unique. Everyone speaks, everyone has something to contribute.

Singing. Following the icebreaker the group usually enters into a period of praise. Sometimes a child chooses or leads the songs; sometimes a parent and child have chosen the songs together. Sometimes a teenager and a college student lead. The praise time may last a few minutes or half an hour, depending upon such factors as the song leaders' choices, the spirit of the group, response to the Sunday morning experiences, or the needs of the evening. Sometimes the praise time turns into a time of lament if someone in the group is suffering a difficult time.

One time after we had finished singing "Jesus, Lamb of God," in the stillness that followed, kindergartner Justin called out in his tiny, high voice, "Can we sing it one more time?" Of course we could, and we sang it with a new sweetness, knowing that Justin was absorbing this beautiful message. Another time our twelve-year-old son (who seldom spoke up) asked if our group could sing Dennis Jernigan's "While You Sing Over Me." Our family owns a copy of this song on tape, but I had never noticed him paying attention when we played it. I certainly hadn't realized that he knew the composer or the name of the song. From that moment on I began to see my son with different eyes. Perhaps some of our spiritual "bricks" are really dormant volcanoes with much happening beneath the surface, awaiting the time to erupt. Worshiping together in a close and intimate setting reveals our inner spiritual lives to our children and theirs to us.

Prayer. We don't usually have long periods of prayer while children are present, but every week we pray for every "family" present—including each college student, not just people who are married with children. One time a man in his early forties who had owned his own business for twenty years took a job working for someone else. He felt he would be less stressed and have more time for family and others. The adults had prayed for him for some weeks as he was making the decision, but as he faced the transition, we prayed together for the whole family.

When a child graduates from high school and leaves to begin a job, attend school, or join the military, we pray for the whole family. When a child enters kindergarten, middle school, junior high, or high school, we pray with and for that child. We know the children in our small group. Usually it takes about six months before a child is comfortable enough to share a specific need to be prayed for by the whole group, but it takes only a few weeks before the children begin to pray for the adults. My own children began to pray for me, even away from the group setting. Ultimately everyone in the group begins to grasp experientially that prayer is the first place one goes—not the last.

Lord's Supper. We have found that observing the Lord's Supper in small groups on Sunday evenings has brought new meaning and depth to the sacrament, especially for children. The children in our church partake of the Lord's Supper with the adults. We have found no biblical prohibition of this practice, which offers the opportunity for children to hear their parents and other adults talk about their feelings and thoughts as they partake of the bread and the cup.

There are dozens of ways to observe communion, and each way reveals a new facet of Christ's death: the Passover, the crucifixion itself, the resurrection, the sacrifice, the atonement, the substitutionary lamb. Here are some of the many ways we have observed the Lord's Supper:

- Have two fathers read the passage in Genesis 22 when God asked Abraham to sacrifice his son, Isaac. Ask the father who read Abraham's part to describe how Abraham must have felt; and ask the father who read God's part to describe how God must have felt when he sacrificed his Son.

- Ask three adults to recall a particularly meaningful communion service and tell why it affected them so much.

- Ask two adults to describe their baptism and the feelings of newness and purity they felt in Christ.

- Ask each person to say what moment of the crucifixion they think was most difficult for Jesus.

- Reenact the last supper with Jesus and his apostles.

Partaking of the Lord's Supper in these diverse ways helps children and adults begin to discern the many facets of Christ's sacrifice. An added benefit is that it becomes more and more natural for families to discuss spiritual things together.

There is at least one other benefit of taking the Lord's Supper in a small group with children participating. During the four years we were with one church, we were a part of five small groups. We always went with the new group when the old group "birthed." In all five groups, the children wanted to serve the Lord's Supper. They took great delight in carrying the platter of bread to the adults and other children in the group. They also viewed with solemnity the task of toting the tray of juice-filled cups. Then they enjoyed taking up the used paper cups. We never experienced a massive tray spill, though many individual juice spills occurred. We discovered the efficacy of white grape juice. In serving, the children participated in the spiritual life of the Christians around them and they were taught.

Once churches begin to think intergenerationally, creative ways to bring the generations together will begin to emerge. One church in the Northwest constructs a large banner each year that depicts symbolically important milestones and spiritual markers of its members: births, baptisms, marriages, deaths, graduations, and special honors members receive. The banners for the last twelve years hang in the foyer of the church where children (and others) can point to special markers in their lives and the lives of others in their community of believers.

Moving to a more age-inclusive approach is a large undertaking. It entails more than "simply being in one place and doing the same thing together"; it is "a mindset . . . in which all belong and interact in faith and worship—a communion of believers."[14]

✳ ✳ ✳

There's no better way for God's people to learn from "more experienced members of the culture" than in intergenerational Christian communities—groups where people of all ages and maturity levels are together living out the essentials of Christianity. In intergenerational communities, children and teens of all ages learn from each other and from adults; adults learn from teens and children. Blessed with a sense of mutuality, everyone benefits from each other; they grow each other up into Christ. "The person has been correspondingly transformed into a practitioner, a newcomer becoming an old-timer, whose changing knowledge, skills, and discourse are part of a developing identity—in short, a member of a community of practice."[15]

Let's go back to another "icebreaker" question our intergenerational small group once started out with: "When you daydream or imagine, what do you see yourself doing?" Among the responses were these:

- I see myself in college, loving it, having a boyfriend. (Jennifer, a teenager)

- I like to imagine myself as an NFL quarterback, winning the Super Bowl! (Kevin, forty-something)

- I'm in the World Series and I hit a home run with bases loaded in the bottom of the ninth and win the game! (Chris, a graduate student)

- I'm always a Ninja Turtle. (Nolan, a fourth grader)

- I'm back in Vietnam, saving the buddies in my platoon. (Carlos, sixty-something)

- I imagine Ben living with us again; he has a good job. We have another baby, a girl. (Jan, thirty-something)

Then it was Cora's turn. Cora is eighty-something; Charlie, her husband of fifty-five years, died a decade ago. She whispers, "I imagine myself in heaven with Jesus; Charlie is there, James [her deceased son] is there, my mother and dad and my sister, Robbie, are there, and then our other children start to join us, and then, their children. And it just goes on and on. I greet each one with open arms and homemade cookies!"

There was a quiet pause. Then Nolan said, "I'll be there too." Jennifer said, "Me too."

And everyone joined in.

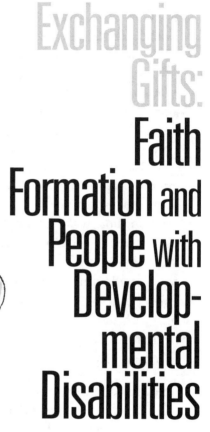

Chapter 10

Exchanging Gifts:
Faith Formation and People with Developmental Disabilities

Erik W. Carter

When I was still in college, I attended a medium-sized church just a few blocks down the street from where I lived. From the outside, the church resembled many of the numerous other churches in that city—a towering steeple, well-manicured landscaping, and a prominent sign out front. From the inside, however, the congregation was quite different from any other church I had attended or visited while growing up. The distinction was found not primarily in the programming and services that church offered, but rather in the community of believers who gathered together each week. Children and adults with developmental disabilities—people who are given labels like Down syndrome, autism, or intellectual disability—were actively involved and integrally woven into the life of this church.

Some of these members sang in the choir, served as greeters or ushers during the worship services, contributed to various ministries, and went on short-term mission trips. Others were primarily involved by attending worship services, church suppers, and fellowship activities. I helped lead an adult Sunday school class that included people with and without disabilities. We gathered together each Sunday during the hour before worship to sing, to learn together, to pray with and for one another, and to catch up on life. For all of us, being together was an important time of fellowship, support, and encouragement.

I recall just how surprised I was when I first learned how far some of my friends with developmental disabilities traveled each Sunday morning to get to that particular church. Most resided one or two towns away, and some lived even farther away. Mentally I began counting the number of churches they passed by on their way to reach this particular church. I came to realize that very few other churches in the area were inviting these individuals to enter into and become a part of their communities. I wondered how many other people with disabilities living in that area struggled to find a church that would welcome them, walk alongside them, and recognize them as essential members of their congregation. I wondered how many people with disabilities and their families—encountering one too many inaccessible or unwelcoming congregations—eventually gave up trying to find a church altogether. And I wondered how many congregations were missing out on the presence, participation, gifts, and faith of people with disabilities.

In the almost fifteen years since I attended that church, I have had the opportunity to live in several different communities throughout the United States. Although the churches in these cities look a little bit different from each other, my conversations with people with disabilities and their families suggest that the landscape still looks very much the same today. Churches like the one I attended during college are still few and far between—they're the exception rather than the rule. Too many people with developmental disabilities continue to live on the peripheries of community life and, unacceptably, this includes faith communities. Too many people with disabilities and their families encounter barriers rather than welcome. And the membership of too many congregations fails to reflect the rich, diverse, and supportive communities they are called to be.

Faith Formation

When invited to contribute a chapter on faith formation for people with disabilities, I initially pondered the need for a separate chapter on this topic. Would such a chapter be redundant or unduly narrow? After all, the issues addressed elsewhere throughout this book are just as relevant for people with developmental disabilities as they are for people who do not share such labels. There is nothing inherently different about the importance of faith in the lives of people with disabilities, the avenues through which their faith is formed and fostered, or the necessity of opportunities to use their gifts and talents within a body of believers. Having a disability—whether intellectual, physical, or emotional—is simply not a reliable predictor of the importance people ascribe to their faith, the manner in which their faith is formed, or the aspirations they hold for their lives and for their churches. The difference lies primarily in the opportunities many children and adults with disabilities have to establish, explore, and express their faith within their churches. In many churches, numerous barriers hinder the meaningful involvement of people with disabilities in the experiences and activities where faith is born, nurtured, strengthened, and shared. The emphasis of this chapter is on the necessity of removing these barriers to faith formation for people with disabilities within congregational life.

The presence of a disability is not itself a barrier to faith. After all, faith is a gift; it is not something that is earned or achieved, or that one must qualify for to receive. But the presence of a disability does increase the likelihood that a person will encounter substantial barriers to accessing activities within the life of the church that are designed to promote faith formation. There is ample evidence to support this assertion. For example, a survey by Harris Interactive and the National Organization on Disability found that 65 percent of people without disabilities said that they attended a church or other place of worship at least once a month. Only 45 percent of people with significant disabilities reported this same level of involvement. This difference of 20 percentage points reflects what often is called a "participation gap."

If you are tempted to attribute this gap to differences in the importance of people's personal faith, think again. In the very same survey, almost exactly the same percentage of people with and without disabilities said their faith was somewhat or very important to them. Faith is just as important an aspect of life for people regardless of whether or not they have a disability. Yet other powerful factors stand in the way of full participation—including barriers of attitude, accessibility, communication, and theology.[1] Churches must be much more intentional and thoughtful about weaving people with developmental disabilities fully into the life of the church—into the activities, programs, experiences, and relationships that promote faith formation.

Much has already been written about the contexts and conditions within which faith may be more likely to grow and be nurtured. Your own faith journey likely includes some of these important elements. I invite you to take a few minutes to reflect on the experiences and relationships that have shaped, sustained, and deepened your own faith. What factors have played a formative role in shaping your understanding of who—and whose—you are? Perhaps your thoughts are immediately drawn to particular moments within corporate worship, your involvement in a small group, your experiences within a certain ministry, your participation in Christian education classes, or your involvement in particular church-sponsored programs such as youth groups, college-age groups, or men's or women's Bible studies. Your thoughts also will likely turn to relationships—to friendships with teachers and ministry leaders who invested in and cared for you, supportive members of the congregation who surrounded you during a particular season of life, or the sense of belonging and acceptance you feel from being part of your congregation. Maybe you recall the times when you first began to discover your God-given gifts and talents or had occasion to share them with others.

The point of this reflection is simple: to help you realize that those kinds of experiences and relationships are no less important for the people with developmental disabilities in your congregation. Certainly we all have our own unique story, and our faith journey has been shaped in myriad ways through our encounters with many different people. But just as we should not assume that there is a single "recipe" for faith formation, neither should we presume that people with disabilities require a set of experiences and relationships that is fundamentally different than those of anyone else. What people with disabilities may need most—indeed, what we all need most—are invitations, encouragement, opportunities, and support to participate meaningfully in the formative experiences churches offer their members.

Elements of Faith Formation

Presence. A church's efforts to encourage and support faith formation for all of the members of its community—with and without disabilities—will bear limited fruit if these members are not present or participating in these experiences. Although this point may seem self-evident and unnecessary to emphasize, a glimpse into the everyday life of most churches suggests that the absence of people with disabilities is one of the first issues that must be considered. A church can develop the most engaging children's programs, the most moving worship experiences, the most elaborate musical programs, the most innovative adult ministries, or the most creative ministry efforts, but if people with disabilities (and other segments of our communities) are not invited to attend, welcomed when they arrive, and supported to participate, the faith formation of a large segment of that community will continue to be overlooked.

It is important to underscore that the absence of people with disabilities from your congregation is not an indicator of their absence from the communities that surround your church. According to the U.S. Census Bureau, there are more than 50 million people with disabilities living in America. That means that approximately 19 percent—about one-fifth—of any particular community fits this description. Now for some basic math— perhaps the last thing you expected to do when cracking open this book. What is one-fifth of the population of your neighborhood, your town, or your city? In a small town of 5,000 people, almost 1,000 children and adults experience some type of disability. In a mid-sized city of 50,000 people, almost 10,000 share this label. And in an urban city of 500,000 people, almost 100,000 people have one or more disabilities. To learn more about the prevalence of disabilities in your community, visit the American FactFinder website (http://factfinder.census.gov) and enter in your city, county, or zip code. Many other countries compile and disseminate similar information.[2]

Such numbers can easily seem abstract, so it may be helpful to consider your own church and the neighborhoods that surround it. The United States Census Bureau reports that more than one-quarter of all families in the United States have at least one relative who experiences some type of disability. In 2000, that came to more than 21 million families. So if your congregation has more than four families, you can safely assume that disability is a reality within your congregation. If people with disabilities are not present in your church's Christian education classes, worship services, small groups, potlucks, and ministry programs, it is not because they are not residing in your community. On average, every fourth or fifth residential door you knock on in the neighborhood that surrounds your church is likely to represent a household that includes at least one member with a disability.

In many churches, then, an essential first step for supporting faith formation involves extending new invitations. The best way to increase the presence of people with disabilities in your congregation is simply to invite them. If you asked members of your congregation to share what brought them through the doors of your church for the first time, most people who did not grow up within the congregation would point to having received a personal invitation. Of course, an announcement on a church sign, newspaper, or website is quite a different thing than a personal invitation. The former only tells people that a particular event is occurring, the latter communicates that their presence really does matter.

Shared experiences. Most churches already offer a wide array of worship, learning, service, and fellowship activities aimed at promoting faith formation among members. Yet when some congregations first decide to more intentionally invite people with developmental disabilities into the life of their church, they often start by establishing separate Sunday school programs or specialized ministries. This may reflect the perception that typical worship services, Sunday school classes, and other activities would be inappropriate or too abstract for persons with an intellectual disability or autism, or that adapting existing activities would prove too burdensome. Yet when a congregation only offers separate programs and activities for people with developmental disabilities, the lives of its members rarely end up intersecting. As a result, what we often call "corporate worship" is not truly corporate—many integral members of our communities are still not present.

I recently read an article describing the successful efforts of one Wisconsin town to build an accessible community playground for *all* children—with and without disabilities. Although the majority of community playgrounds are entirely inaccessible to children with physical disabilities, a few are retrofitted with special equipment or separate accessible sections are added. Such adaptations reflect a nod to inclusion, but children with disabilities still can only access a sliver of activities and may not be able to play with all the other children. This particular playground was intended to be different. It was a "universally designed" playground—one planned from the very outset with every child in mind, one that would enable all children to truly play and spend time together. One of the leaders of the project explained, "People used to ask, 'Why do you want to build a playground just for children with disabilities?' . . . They didn't get it. It's only when you build a playground for children with disabilities that you build one for all children."[3]

Churches are called to adopt the same perspective. They should design programs and services with a much broader vision of community in mind. If churches develop their Sunday school program's activities for children with disabilities at the outset, they will likely discover that these experiences are more engaging and enjoyable for all children. If churches design their buildings to be accessible to people with physical and sensory disabilities, they will discover that they end up with facilities that are easier for everyone to navigate, regardless of whether or not they have a disability. If churches learn to do a good job of welcoming people with developmental disabilities into the life of the church, they will quickly discover that they have also learned something fundamental about how to show hospitality to anyone who feels like a stranger in their community. The recurring lesson of efforts to promote inclusion in schools, workplaces, and communities is that such efforts really are good for everyone.

Relationships and belonging. Our faith tends to deepen and grow when we spend time in the company and companionship of others who share our faith. Through our relationships with one another and the activities we share, we learn to worship, to pray, to sing, to support one another, and to be faithful. This is true irrespective of whether someone has a disability. But this is precisely where people with developmental disabilities encounter considerable barriers.[4] Sometimes architectural barriers stifle opportunities to develop and maintain relationships. Inaccessible facilities can prevent some people with disabilities from entering a classroom, sitting with friends during worship services, singing in the choir alongside others, attending a small group in members' homes, or participating meaningfully in other church-sponsored activities. Others experience attitudinal barriers. For example, some members may have limited knowledge about or prior encounters with people with disabilities, increasing their hesitation or reluctance to initiate a conversation or extend an invitation. As a result, some people with developmental disabilities never really feel like they are a part of the life of a congregation, and they experience few true friendships.

Creating supportive opportunities for people with and without developmental disabilities to get to know one another and experience a sense of connection to and belonging within the community of believers is a central task of the church. Church leaders should take steps to promote broader awareness and greater understanding of disabilities within their congregation. At the same time, individual members should be encouraged to step outside their usual relationship circles and make efforts to get to know and spend time with people with developmental disabilities in their faith community.

An easy starting point would simply involve saying hello before church, sitting together in Sunday school or during worship services, sharing a hymnal, serving together as ushers, joining a small group together, or sharing a few minutes of conversation during the social hour. It is important that everyone in the church feels welcome and known for two or three hours on a Sunday morning. But it is also essential to remember that there are seven days in the week, not just one. Life continues on for everyone—including people with developmental disabilities—following the benediction and after the coffee and doughnuts are all packed up. When people leave their church buildings on Sunday mornings, they should, in a sense, be all leaving together. This means remaining present in each others' lives beyond the walls of the congregation—checking in on each other during the week, sharing a meal, finding out how work and life are going, or just spending time together. Such intentional and sustained connections can be instrumental in the lives of people with developmental disabilities, as they are for all of us.

Exchanging gifts. Everyone has found themselves on the receiving end of some kind of assistance or support at some point in their adult lives. Perhaps you have had an illness or injury, or you experienced challenging times. During these seasons of life, you likely turned to family, neighbors, or church members for help. But few of you reside exclusively in that place of "recipient"—known only for your position of need and rarely thought of for what you have to give and contribute.

Contrast this with the way many people with developmental disabilities are viewed and treated within the life of the church and in society at large. Churches often talk about disabilities within the context of ministry to people with disabilities, outreach to people with disabilities, or service to people with disabilities. Rarely do these conversations emphasize ministry with or by people with disabilities.[5] People with disabilities are often viewed as the focus of ministry rather than as believers who have essential gifts and talents just waiting to be shared with others. The gifts of people with disabilities are too often overlooked in our churches. Yet serving others and sharing gifts is an important avenue through which faith can grow.

In the fifth chapter of this book, Robert Keeley offers the reminder that "people of all ages need to feel they have an important place in our church community." We all experience times in our lives when we need support, encouragement, and assistance from others. Despite the high value placed on independence in our culture, most of us would acknowledge that we are interdependent. Just as we all can benefit from the gifts and service of others, the corollary is also true—we have all been given gifts and talents that are needed by someone else. The apostle Paul writes, "Each person is given something to do that shows who God is: Everyone gets in on it, everyone benefits. All kinds of things are handed out by the Spirit, and to all kinds of people! The variety is wonderful..." (1 Cor. 12:4-7, *The Message*). These gifts come without qualifiers or exceptions. The presence of a developmental disability does not mean a person does not receive essential gifts to share, nor does it mean that others have no need for those gifts. One important task of the church is to help its members discover their gifts and to employ them within and beyond the walls of the church. People with developmental disabilities should be given the encouragement and support to use their gifts in the service of others within the church.

The opportunity that lies before your congregation is to become a community that invites, encourages, and supports the meaningful participation of people with developmental disabilities and their families in the life of your church.

Chapter 11

Growing in Wisdom and Stature:

Recent Research on Spirituality and Faith Formation

Kevin E. Lawson

God created us as holistic persons with physical and spiritual natures that can grow and develop as we move through childhood, adolescence, and our adult years. Scripture reflects this perspective with respect to Jesus himself: "As Jesus grew up, he increased in wisdom and in favor with God and people" (Luke 2:52). Like Jesus, our lives are to be characterized by growth—mentally, physically, spiritually, and relationally.

But how do people grow spiritually? Should we expect a predictable pattern, or is it all a mystery? While research in human development has provided helpful insights on the ways people change and grow throughout their lives—insights that can help guide ministry efforts—there are legitimate questions regarding whether or not this kind of research can help us understand spiritual growth.

Human spirituality and faith formation have not always received a lot of attention in the fields of human development and church ministry. On the one hand, some researchers in human development have tended to avoid the topics of religion, spirituality, and faith, viewing them as outside the focus of modern research. On the other hand, leaders in church ministry have at times been skeptical of the study of spirituality, viewing it as the realm of the Holy Spirit and not subject to typical patterns of growth. Today more research is being done on this neglected area of human experience, and as a result, we are learning more about the spiritual lives of children, youth, and adults. Recent research has taken a number of approaches. Some researchers have focused on what is often termed "religiosity," dealing with issues of beliefs, behaviors, and participation in religious activities. Others have focused on a person's concept of God, sense of spiritual well-being (in relationship with God and others), aspects of spiritual maturity, or personal spiritual experience.

This field of research is still fairly new, and we have much more to learn. While we will never fully understand how God works in the human soul, we can gain insights that can help us develop congregational ministries that promote spiritual vitality and growth toward maturity. The more we know about the people we minister to and what impacts their spiritual lives, the wiser we can be in our ministry efforts.

Learning About the Spirituality and Faith Formation of Children

In the late twentieth century, research on the spiritual lives of children tended to focus on cognitive development issues such as how children develop their concepts of God, how they understand death or prayer, and when they might be ready for learning more challenging spiritual concepts such as the doctrine of the Trinity. While this research has been helpful for curriculum developers and teachers in the church context, recent research has focused more on the spiritual lives and experiences of children and how they grow into their own faith, not just learn about it from their parents or church. This new focus takes seriously the inherent spiritual nature of children as created in the image of God. Researchers including Robert Coles,[1] David Hay and Rebecca Nye,[2] Robert Wuthnow,[3] Brendan Hyde,[4] and many others have sought to gain insight into the spiritual experiences of children and how this influences their lives as they grow. Their efforts have helped us better understand the critical importance of childhood as a time of genuine spiritual experience, laying foundations that will influence spiritual growth in later years. Following are several research findings and their implications for ministry practice:

Children have an inherent spiritual awareness and genuine spiritual experiences. Researchers such as Hay and Nye and Hyde have approached their research with children with a fairly broad understanding of spirituality. Though their perspective on spirituality may not adequately represent Christian faith commitments, their research does show that children are not empty, passive vessels to be filled with religious instruction. Instead children are active agents with spiritual awareness of their own, trying to make sense of their experiences and what they are taught. Spirituality is not something that happens later in life but is a part of human experience throughout our lives, and should be taken seriously at all ages. Too often in the church context we view children as "not yet ready for prime time." Perhaps because they don't have the vocabulary to talk about it well, we don't expect children to have spiritual experiences or to be spiritually sensitive. Recent research challenges us to take the spirituality of children seriously instead of dismissing it because it is not as "mature" as that of adults.

Parents are not only "first teachers" of their children; they also impact how children relate with God. Research by Bowlby, Ainsworth, and others on childhood "attachment theory" has explored how children develop relationships with their caregivers that in turn allow them to deal with stressful situations, explore their surroundings, and develop other supportive relationships. A major focus of this research is on the importance of developing a relationship with a primary caregiver for normal emotional and social growth. While this research has primarily focused on human relationships, some have explored how the different attachment patterns that children develop with their caregivers may impact the kind of "attachment" they develop with God. The theory is that early childhood experiences carry over to how we view God and our relationship with him. If children's caregivers are not sensitive and responsive to them, if children do not feel secure, it is harder for them to trust in God's care for them or to feel secure in God. Parents and other caregivers have an impact on how secure children feel with the God who created them and loves them. Our incarnation of the love of God is critical for their growing relationship with him.

Children experience the faith of their parents and learn as apprentices in the normal activities of life. John Westerhoff[5] presents a model of faith development that uses the image of the rings of a tree, with the inner rings continuing to exert an influence even as other rings grow around them. In his model, children are described as first "experiencing" the faith of their parents as they are cared for and included in their religious involvements. Later they grow into an "affiliative" faith as they participate in both family religious activities and faith community activities (worship, instruction, fellowship, service). This perspective highlights the importance of children's ongoing participation in family and church activities. Children are always learning, not just when we are officially teaching them, and their participation in family and church is like an apprenticeship in the faith. For good or ill, children pick up and learn from what is really happening, not just what we say is important. Parents who live out what they teach and who show integrity in their speech and actions have a deep impact on the growing faith of their children. Wuthnow's research with Christians and Jews demonstrates the powerful impact of childhood religious experiences on the later religious commitments and faith of adults. The important question for us is, what do children experience in our faith communities, and what is it teaching them?

Children attempt to make meaning of all they experience—including spiritual experiences and religious instruction. Recent research on the spiritual lives of children reveals their active efforts at understanding and interpreting what they experience and are taught. They are not passive recipients content to parrot back what they hear. This came out one morning when my son was eight and I was making pancakes for breakfast. We were alone in the kitchen and he said, "Dad, I don't think you want to hear this, but I'm not sure I believe the Bible is true." When I asked why, Nate replied, "I just don't see how dinosaurs and the Bible can both be true." This led to a great conversation about dinosaur fossils, archaeology, and how dinosaurs fit into the whole creation story. At the end, he seemed relieved that it was possible to believe in both dinosaurs and what the Bible says about God's work of creation.

Like my son, other children are taking in lots of information and experiences that are not always easy to put together into a coherent whole. They need help from others in sorting through the issues, gaining important missing information, challenging some of what they have learned, and seeing how it all fits together.

It's important to listen to children, allowing time for sharing experiences and questions and paying attention to the heart. The research findings we've looked at so far make one thing very clear: it is critically important that we take time to listen to our children in order to understand what is happening in their spiritual lives. We must have opportunities to share our faith and spiritual experiences together, and we must encourage our children to raise questions about the things that concern them. Only then can we discern the kind of spiritual guidance and instruction our children need. This is one reason why parents will always have the major opportunity for nurturing and guiding the spiritual lives of their children—if they take it. Church settings are simply not as conducive for children to raise their burning questions as a leisurely breakfast on a Saturday morning. What are we doing to help parents seize the opportunities they have to guide the spiritual growth of their children?

But even in the church setting, as we create teaching ministries for children, we must be attentive to how children are processing what they are learning. We must allow time to listen to *their* questions, not just have them answer *our* questions. Recognizing that spiritual growth is not just a matter of the head but also of the heart, we must pay attention to the affective aspects of our children's faith, not just their cognitive understanding.

Rituals, holidays, family time, reading, praying, and serving are formative experiences. Wuthnow's research of adults reflecting on their childhood experiences highlights the deep impact that family and church rituals, holiday celebrations, and worship observances can have in the lives of children. These experiences can teach in informal ways, reinforcing important aspects of the faith we are encouraging our children to grow into. The full life of the church, including how we celebrate weddings, carry out funerals, and celebrate Christmas and Easter, has the potential to shape the faith of our children. We need to pay more attention to what our children experience in these events and what this teaches them. Similarly, spending time with parents or caregivers reading Bible stories, praying, and serving the needs of others has a deep impact on how children grow in their understanding of the Christian faith and how it makes a difference in their relationship with God and others.

These six areas help us begin to understand the vital importance of childhood as a time of spiritual experience and formation. Church leaders must be attentive to this critical time and promote strong spiritual practices both at home and in the church community.

Learning About the Spirituality and Faith Formation of Youth

In recent years a number of studies have sought to understand the spiritual lives of youth and how their religious participation impacts other aspects of their lives. Major national research efforts such as the National Study of Youth and Religion (NSYR) and multitudes of smaller studies have provided much insight into how the spirituality and religious experiences of adolescence is both similar to and different from childhood. Some studies have addressed how religious participation impacts a variety of "at risk" behaviors such as drug use, sexual activity, and school performance. Others have focused on the impact of parents, youth groups, peers, and adult mentors on the religious commitments and practices of youth. These studies and many more have shed light on how the church can respond in ministry to youth in ways that foster a growing, vital faith.

Here are some of the critical issues raised by this research:

Youth is a time of transition and personalizing of faith commitments. According to Westerhoff's model of faith formation, adolescence begins a time of transition in which young people examine more closely the faith they received and experienced in childhood. During this time of "searching faith," adolescents strive to sort out what they have received in childhood and move increasingly to an "owned faith" where they can personally own their religious convictions. This transition takes time and can be an uncomfortable process. Not all congregations or parents are prepared to assist youth through this period of questioning experience. Not all young people work through this at the same time or in the same way, nor do they all experience this as a time of great stress. It's important for parents and church leaders to understand the transition that is happening and to provide contexts where youth can work through their questions without feeling condemned or guilty.

Most youth say that their faith is important to them, but it is fairly vague, with limited impact. Christian Smith and Melinda Lundquist Denton,[6] along with other researchers at the University of North Carolina at Chapel Hill, have undertaken a major longitudinal study of the religious and spiritual lives of American teens. To date, this study has shared two strong findings for the majority of adolescents: first, their faith is important to them, and that faith is fairly consistent with what they have been taught and experienced within their faith communities. Second, at this point in their lives, their faith is fairly vague and personally oriented—what Smith and Denton call "moralistic therapeutic deism." It is a "feel good" religion that makes few claims on them but enables them to pursue a good life. This provides both a wonderful opportunity and a challenge for parents and ministry leaders: opportunity in that young people are open to the importance of faith for their lives, and challenge in determining how to reshape this caricature of faith into a faith that is biblically grounded.

Parents continue to have a major impact on the spiritual lives of their adolescent children, but other adults and peers have a growing impact. Smith and Denton, the Search Institute, and others who carry out research on the spiritual lives of adolescents all report that parents continue to exercise the dominant influence on youth. What they teach their adolescent children, and what they themselves model in expression of their faith (beliefs, attitudes, values, actions), all continue to have an impact as their children grow toward adulthood. At the same time, youth are interacting with more adults in their churches (ministers, lay leaders), schools (teachers), communities (coaches, employers, other parents), and in the media (musicians, sports figures). These adults, especially those who form close relationships with youth, can also have a strong influence on their attitudes, commitments, and behaviors. In addition, this is a time when peer relationships are growing in importance and influence for all aspects of life, including the religious and spiritual. When close friends participate in church and share similar beliefs and values, this reinforces what youth are hearing from their parents and other influential adults.

Youth benefit most from being engaged in the faith, not just learning about it. Research on the impact of service learning, including short-term mission trips and other intensive ministry opportunities, reveals that these stretching experiences can be a great stimulus to a growing faith. It is not enough to teach youth about the faith or to encourage them to believe and do certain things. When youth participate in activities that allow them to express and challenge their faith, they have an opportunity to "taste and see" what it is like to follow and trust God. For many youth these kinds of experiences are a "reality check" for what they really believe. But experience in itself is not enough. Research on the impact of service learning indicates that how youth are prepared for these experiences and the kind of debriefing that follows can make the difference between an interesting experience and a transformative one. The point is to give youth the chance to put their faith into practice and to help them reflect on what God has been teaching them through that experience.

Churches can foster a climate that encourages a growing faith. I mentioned above that adolescence can be a time of transition in faith experience. It can begin a time when young people question the faith they received and developed in childhood to determine if it is sound enough to build their life on. But where will youth have the opportunity to do this kind of questioning and sifting? Reflecting on effective educational ministry practice, Eugene Roehlkepartain[7] talks about the importance of churches fostering a "thinking climate" in their ministry with youth. This includes a warm, welcoming atmosphere and a safe environment where youth can raise questions, voice doubts, and wonder about what they have been taught and what they see happening in the world. In many cases youth need an opportunity to unlearn things they thought they understood as children, or develop better reasons for believing things they have accepted without question. This helps them grow into an "owned faith" that is strong enough to guide life decisions and commitments. While this process of "owning" faith will not be completed in adolescence, it is important that it be allowed to begin. If not, youth may either leave the church and discard their faith as irrelevant or retreat into a compartmentalized, nominal faith that has little impact on the rest of their lives.

Both peer groups and intergenerational experiences are important. One phenomena of contemporary church life is an increasing age segregation of worship and learning experiences in many congregations. While this provides opportunities for ministries that are targeted to the needs of particular age groups, it limits the kind of cross-generational relationships that can be critical for encouraging youth to stay connected with the church community when they graduate from high school. Wes Black[8] reports that having relationships with non-parent adults in church provides youth with opportunities for supportive friendships, mentoring, advice, and counsel, and having these relationships encourages ongoing church involvement beyond high school. This "both-and" dimension becomes more critical as youth approach the end of high school and transition to young adulthood. Connections to the larger church, including using their gifts in worship leadership and various other ministries within and outside the church, help youth see themselves as part of the larger body of Christ made up of people in many ages and stages of life.

Learning about the Spirituality and Faith Formation of Adults

In the later part of the twentieth century, James Fowler conducted research on faith development and proposed a model of faith developing in stages.[9] This theory has stirred up interest in spiritual growth over the course of adulthood. Since then, a range of research has been carried out to better understand what kinds of experiences promote spiritual growth for adults. Some of the issues addressed in this research include an examination of how adults continue to develop and learn, the importance of both church ministries and individual spiritual practices, the impact of small groups, and why religious activity alone is not an adequate measure of spiritual maturity.

Adulthood continues to be a time of changes, new challenges, and opportunities for spiritual growth. Research in human development has helped us better appreciate the dynamic nature of adulthood. As adults age and experience new demands and challenges, many of the issues they face change. Marriage, parenting, vocational changes, aging parents, retirement, aging, and deaths in the family all bring new questions and new opportunities for the church to show how God cares for people and gives their lives meaning and direction. Recognizing that adulthood is not a static time, churches need to be aware of and responsive to the challenges adults are facing and the opportunities that come for spiritual renewal and growth.

Adults learn differently from children, requiring a different type of teaching for spiritual growth. The field of adult education has grown over the last few decades, bringing an increasing awareness of how adults learn and what they are looking for when they participate in learning experiences. This study of "andragogy" by people like Malcolm Knowles[10] and K. Patricia Cross[11] highlights the intrinsic motivation that draws adults to a learning experience, the life experience they interact with as they learn new things, and the importance of practical application. Adults bring their experiences into the learning process and have the potential to engage in an interactive learning process. This means that our preaching and teaching can help adults examine their faith and spiritual lives and consider where God might be challenging them to further growth in faithfulness.

Small group ministries can provide a powerful context for spiritual growth and life change. Robert Wuthnow[12] and others have found that small groups can be powerful contexts for adults seeking to learn, examine their lives, and begin to change as God challenges and teaches them. Small groups come in many types, addressing various needs such as recovery, Bible study, prayer, personal care, evangelism, and the like. In church settings, small groups have become a major ministry model for encouraging spiritual growth. Greg Hawkins and Cally Parkinson[13] also identify small groups as a powerful catalyst for spiritual growth, especially for those who are fairly new in the faith or who are looking to grow into a closer walk with Christ. Small groups provide a context for addressing questions, troubleshooting problems, and receiving feedback and encouragement as participants try new behaviors in obedience to God.

The importance and impact of church activities and individual spiritual practices changes as adults mature in their faith. While restricted in scope, recent research by Hawkins and Parkinson at Willow Creek has stirred a lot of interest in how what helps adults grow spiritually changes as they mature in their faith. This ongoing study challenges church leaders to better appreciate how involvement in small groups, worship services, spiritual friendships, and service in the church can help bring seekers into a new and growing relationship with Christ. While many of these things continue to be influential as new believers grow, adult education, opportunities to serve others, relationships with spiritual mentors, and sharing their faith with others helps promote a closer relationship with Christ. But personal spiritual practices are also important, especially developing habits of Bible study and reflection, prayer, and solitude to listen to God. Those who plan and lead adult ministries in the church need to understand how the impact of these catalysts for spiritual growth changes over time in order to help those who are fairly mature in their faith continue to grow and not stagnate or disconnect from their church community.

We must not mistake religious activity for spiritual growth and maturity. Janet Hagberg and Robert Guelich reflect on six typical stages in people's spiritual lives.[14] The first three characterize new and growing Christians who benefit most from strong group involvement, both in receiving instruction from others and in serving others. The latter three characterize people who have been growing and productive, but who have run into challenges of faith and life that do not conform to their earlier understanding. These people need to go on a more inward journey of spiritual seeking to work through the questions and issues they face. It is tempting to assume that someone who is involved in church ministry and actively engaged in the life of the church must be doing well spiritually. While this may be the case, religious activities can become an escape or a façade masking spiritual stagnation or decline. When we try to assess the needs for spiritual growth within our congregations, we cannot assume that all active people are doing well spiritually. In some cases, continued spiritual growth may require reducing group commitments to make room for more individual pursuits, such as spiritual direction, retreats, and solitude that can provide stimulus for renewed spiritual vitality and growth.

The insights from current research on the spiritual lives of children, youth, and adults do not provide a formula for growth, nor do they ignore the sovereign work of the Holy Spirit in people's lives. But they do help us better appreciate the dynamic of spiritual life at different ages. They can help us understand the kinds of needs people have and the kinds of ministry approaches that may be beneficial. May God grant you and those you minister with the wisdom both to understand the unique needs of those in your congregation and how to respond to those needs in ways that encourage ongoing spiritual vitality and growth.

Chapter 12

Questioning
the "Right"
Answers:
Faith
Formation
in the
Postmodern
Matrix

David M. Csinos

There is a time for everything. . . .

—Ecclesiastes 3:1

Postmodernism has become a buzzword in Western culture, and the meanings given to it weigh it down with baggage and taboos. Some see postmodernism as a threat to the world at large. Others believe that it directly challenges Christianity. Still others embrace this movement and wish to see it come to full fruition. For many people, however, postmodernism is a confusing word filled with complex meaning.

Postmodernism is a broad movement, or collection of movements, that does not lend itself to being defined. But it can be *described*, and one person who has attempted such a description is Brian McLaren. According to McLaren, postmodernism is a reaction to the modernism[1] that the world has passed through and by which it has been affected. Rather than being anti-modernism, postmodernism is, in a more accurate sense, after-modernism.

Without trying to define postmodernism, let me sketch out a few of its key aspects.[2] As I do so, you'll see that central to postmodernism is a hermeneutic of suspicion;[3] that is, postmodernists are skeptical of the truths, stories, and understandings of the world that have been held up by modernism, such as the inevitability of human progress and the inherent goodness of knowledge.

From Me to We

The modernism that dominated the West (and Western Christianity) for the past few centuries has been thoroughly individualistic. The free individual was seen as the "base ingredient" of culture.[4] Postmodernism responds to this by focusing on communities in which individuals participate and the ways in which people are influenced by those around them. Postmodernism affirms the communal nature of humanity both geographically (in specific places) and temporally (at specific times).[5]

The Enlightenment (around 1650-1800), which is seen as the mother of modernism, held that the West is the world's most advanced civilization and that "all of humankind would eventually come to appreciate and strive to attain the benefits of the Western ideal."[6] Postmodernism challenges this view. The rise of technology and globalization has allowed people around the world to communicate with one another. This in turn caused people to question the assumption that the West is the pinnacle of civilization. An example of this mindset is seen in Michael Moore's popular documentaries.[7]

Since postmodernism does not see the West as the best civilization, it encourages pluralism.[8] Along with pluralism comes a recognition that there are multiple realities in the world, and, in the words of psychologist Barbara Rogoff, "there is not likely to be One Best Way"[9] or one best culture. Rather than suggesting that our society be a melting pot in which all cultures conform to a homogenous monoculture, postmodernism encourages communities to become tossed salads—heterogenous collections of multiple cultures. This diversity can also be seen in the eclectic style of postmodern art, the most popular form being the collage, which juxtaposes several styles on one canvas. Collages reflect what some believe to be the "central hallmark" of postmodernity: the coexistence and affirmation of multiple cultures and forms of cultural expression.[10] This affirmation of pluralism has significant implications for many of the core values of postmodernism, especially views of truth.

The (Relative) Truth about Truths

In *Jesus Christ Superstar*, Pilate asks Jesus a postmodern question: "What are truths? Are mine the same as yours?"[11] As a result of the Enlightenment's focus on reason and science, modernism became associated with the study of objective truth, that is, universal facts that are absolutely true in all times and places. By studying the world as unbiased, objective observers, modernists believed that truth consisted only of what could be discovered through reason.

Postmodernism challenges this view by positing that even if objective truths exist, human beings cannot know them, for we all possess metaphorical lenses through which we see the world—lenses made up of subjective past experiences, knowledge, and feelings. Since we cannot rid ourselves of these lenses and become impartial observers of the world, postmodernism suggests that we can never discover objective, absolute truths. In the words of Tony Jones, postmodernism acknowledges "that all our conversations about reality involve layers of limited perception and human interpretation, and are therefore open to question and correction."[12]

This, however, does not mean that there is no truth; rather, what counts as truth changes as one moves from modernism to postmodernism. "There are other valid paths to knowledge besides reason, say the postmoderns, including the emotions and the intuition."[13] Postmodernism recognizes that truths are constructed by human beings and are highly contextual and communal.[14] First, truths are contextual because, rather than being ahistorical, they reflect the particular situations in which people find themselves. Language alone makes truths contextual, for language is a human construction that can never perfectly reflect the concepts that it describes.[15] Second, truths are communal because they depend on the community that professes them and they are relative to its worldview. A truth, for postmoderns, is not for all people and all times. It is relative to one's community, and, since there are many contexts and communities in the world, there are many possible truths.[16] With all this in mind, Pilate's question could be slightly changed to more accurately reflect postmodernism: "What are truths? Are ours the same as yours?"[17]

Deconstructing Deconstruction

Let's carry our discussion of truth further as we examine another important aspect of postmodernism: *deconstruction*. A term not to be confused with *destruction* nor *un-construction*, deconstruction is a practice and theory that seeks to take apart, or deconstruct, a cultural product or discipline in order to examine how it is constructed and thus better understand the concepts and ideas that constitute it.[18] In Brian McLaren's words, "Deconstruction is not destruction, as many erroneously assume, but rather careful and loving attention to the construction of ideas, beliefs, systems, values, and cultures."[19] It seeks to reveal social constructions for what they are: human interpretations of the world. Again, whether or not

there are inherent truths in the world, postmodernism affirms that
we, as finite beings, cannot fully grasp them.

Richard Middleton and Brian Walsh describe deconstruction by
placing it as a response to the Western "metaphysics of presence,"
a phrase that speaks of the Western habit of seeing our views of
the world as accurate descriptions of reality.[20] Sometimes our
conceptualizations actually define what is real. Deconstruction
tries to demonstrate that "what is claimed to be present [or real]
is really absent and that the given is itself a construction of human
discourse."[21] By deconstructing a given "reality," we can see that
what we label as real and true are simply our understandings of
what is real and true, our constructed interpretations of reality.

Language, the primary medium through which we construct and
interpret reality, is at the heart of deconstruction.[22] "Language
is the necessary filter through which the world comes to us."[23]
Although we interpret the world through language, most of us use
language without seeing it as a tool, as a means of interpretation.[24]
Deconstruction helps us take apart our linguistically-constructed
understandings of reality and expose them for what they are:
interpretations.

Although some people see deconstruction in a negative light,
Jacques Derrida, who famously wrote, "There is nothing outside the
text," claimed that deconstruction, or seeing what is embedded in
the text, is positive and constructive.[25] We deconstruct in order to
better understand ourselves and others. Deconstruction is positive
because "all our experience is already an interpretation."[26] We
cannot do anything without interpreting it; deconstruction helps us
to recognize this.

Let's go back to our discussion of truth. Instead of proving that there
is no truth, deconstruction alters our understanding of what counts
as truth. "The fact that it is a matter of interpretation does not mean
that an interpretation cannot be true or a good interpretation."[27]
Human beings can know truth through recognizing that all human
experience is interpretive, and by deconstructing interpretations

to better understand them. Rather than resting on objectivity and universalism (it is true for all times and places), the truth of an interpretation rests on the common interpretations and narratives of one's community.

Metanarrative

Human beings are influenced by the stories that we tell ourselves and those told about us. For example, many people in the West are influenced by the story of consumerism, which says that whoever dies with the most toys wins. Such narratives provide frameworks for human living:

> In order to understand our world, to make sense of our lives, and to make our most important decisions about how we ought to be living, we depend on some story. . . . Individual experiences make sense and acquire meaning only when seen within the context or frame of some story we believe to be the true story of the world.[28]

Metanarratives are the large stories that "claim to be able to legitimate or prove the story's claim by an appeal to universal reason."[29] Modernism was greatly concerned with metanarratives, holding that these overarching stories are true because any rational person can see that they are so.

The postmodern philosopher Jean-François Lyotard wrote that postmodernism is "incredulity toward metanarratives,"[30] or disbelief of the big stories proven true by reason. Since postmoderns hold that truth is relative to one's community and all human knowledge is interpretation, they hold that modern metanarratives are false. Reason alone, they suggest, cannot prove a story's universal truth. What is more, this whole understanding of metanarratives is itself a metanarrative: only those who are part of the narrative that believes reason alone defines (objective) truth can affirm that metanarratives are true because reason proves they are true.[31] Thus, the entire understanding of metanarratives betrays itself because it too is simply a narrative.

While postmodernism challenges metanarratives for their appeal to reason, it recognizes that all knowledge is grounded in narrative.[32] But who is to know which narrative is the right one, if there is such a right narrative? This is what Lyotard has called "the problem of legitimation."[33] Since no one possesses a God's-eye view of the world, we can never know which, if any, narrative is the truest.

But this does not mean that there are no true narratives. Post-modernism, if you will remember, says that truth is relative to one's community; a narrative is true in relation to the community that holds it. This is often a difficult concept for people to reconcile. One may ask: Does this mean that the narrative of the Nazi party is just as valid as that of the Christian church? Speaking very broadly, yes, because postmodernism holds that no human community can definitely claim to know an ultimate narrative of the world. Yet both are equally invalid if they claim to be The Metanarrative of the world (as did Hitler and as do many Christian groups). This is where deconstruction comes into play: by deconstructing narratives, we can better understand how the narratives that communities tell themselves are not true for all people and at all times.

Faith Formation in the Postmodern Matrix

So what does all of this have to do with faith formation? After all, this is a book about faith formation—not postmodernism. I believe that this new, postmodern world in which we find ourselves has implications for how Christians are formed in faith. For too long, Christians have been steeped in modernist understandings of the world; it is time that we continue to move forward and explore new ways of engaging in faith formation in the postmodern matrix. While some people see postmodernism as antithetical to the (modernist) church, I, along with others, believe that postmodernism can be a catalyst for the church to recover its authentic mission—to be the people of God.[34] In what follows, I offer eight ways for the church to engage in authentic faith formation in the postmodern world. While this list is not exhaustive, it is a good place to start thinking about what implications postmodernism has for the global and local faith community.

Faith formation in the postmodern matrix is communal. Postmodernism challenges individualism by recognizing that people exist in communities. Thus, faith formation in the postmodern era is highly communal and recognizes the faith community's shaping influence on its members. Formation is no longer about forming an individual person, but forming a member of a community that will, in turn, influence the wider world. In the postmodern world, all people have the power to form one another's faith.

In an essay cowritten with Dan Jennings, Brian McLaren, and Karen Marie Yust, we argued that faith communities ought to be the primary community of influence on its members.[35] Postmodernism recognizes that people exist in multiple communities that compete with one another for primary influence. Since one's faith can be formed by anyone (often we aren't aware that this is happening), Christian faith communities ought to see that they should not be simply one of a multitude of voices; they need to be the primary voice and the most significant influence on the faith formation of its members.

Faith formation in the postmodern matrix affirms and encourages diversity. Postmodernism "embraces more than just tolerance for other practices and viewpoints: it affirms and celebrates diversity."[36] Thus, faith formation amidst postmodernism affirms and celebrates diversity; as Morgan Freeman's character in the film *Robin Hood* says, "[God] loves wondrous variety."[37] Postmodernism affirms that there are many ways of being Christian and being formed in the faith.

The Christian faith community is a *glocalized* community—that is, it is global and local. Glocalization affirms that globalization includes "worldwide processes adapted to local circumstances."[38] The worldwide phenomenon that sweeps across the Christian church is the narrative of God—the gospel—manifested in diverse ways and through practices across the globe. While formation occurs primarily in local faith communities, postmodernism reminds us that our community's ways of being Christian are not the only ways, for there is no one best way. Rather than treating faith formation as though it were a massive baking project producing millions of "cookie-cutter" Christians, postmodernism reminds us that faith formation need not be uniform; after all, we have much to learn from one another.

Faith formation in the postmodern matrix raises questions about how different realities coexist. This diversity raises a question that is central to faith formation in a postmodern world: How can several diverse realities peacefully coexist?[39] This is a question many people have wrestled with. It has been asked at the micro level (for example, at Immanuel Mennonite Church, a multiethnic congregation in Virginia) and at the macro level (for example, in Canada, one of the world's most multicultural nations). Faith formation involves the quest to find constructive answers to this question.

Without assuming to have the solution, let me offer two tips that can aid Christians in finding an answer. First, we should move from tolerance to the celebration of diversity. Second, we can engage in honest and open dialogue with people from different cultures. My friend Jerry and I regularly engage in such conversation. I am a Caucasian from Ontario and Jerry is an African American from North Carolina, and we continually seek to understand one another. Along the way we make mistakes and say the wrong things—but this is where the remarkable power of forgiveness is manifested.

Faith formation in the postmodern matrix focuses on faith. The apostle Paul wrote: "We walk by faith, not by sight" (2 Cor. 5:7, NRSV). This has significant meaning for faith formation in a postmodern world, for it challenges the inevitability of progress through human reason and truth based on reason. Thus, progress in faith ought to be about faith instead of reason. While faith is not unreasonable, faith does not depend on reason. Postmodernism affirms that we cannot fully understand God and that belief is an act of faith, not reason. What it means to know God changes from knowing *about* God to knowing God as we know a friend. We don't know all about our friends, but we still know them in intimate ways. Although knowledge about God can help us to know God, faith formation in a postmodern world reinforces the importance of faith practices as well. Such formation values the ancient spiritual practices and disciplines—like fasting and contemplative prayer—as ways to better know God.[40]

Faith formation in the postmodern matrix is about the active production of meaning. The contemporary, capitalistic world sees people as consumers. We consume food, products, and entertainment. Many contemporary (modernist) churches see congregants as consumers as they invite them to sit in theater seating and ingest Christian music, drama, and preaching. Such settings teach people to consume Christianity.

Postmodernism affirms that human beings are not simply consumers; we are also producers. And one thing that we produce is meaning. Faith formation, which values knowing God over knowing about God, does not involve what Paolo Freire calls the banking model of education, "an act of depositing, in which . . . the teacher issues communiqués and makes deposits which the students patiently receive, memorize, and repeat."[41] Rather, postmodern faith formation encourages people to actively make meaning for themselves. One of the primary tools for such meaning-making is the Bible, which is a collage of different interpretations of God's interactions with humanity. Furthermore, this formation celebrates a questioning faith that acknowledges that all people doubt, that no one has the right answers, and that we can learn from one another.

Faith formation in the postmodern matrix is hopeful. Postmodernism can be pessimistic.[42] It challenges the assumption that knowledge is good, rejects the inevitability of human progress, and exposes oppression and violence through deconstruction.

The gospel, on the other hand, is inherently hopeful. It speaks of justice, peace, and love. It offers reconciliation, forgiveness, and hope that God has not abandoned us. It reminds us, "If God is for us, who is against us?" (Rom. 8:31, NRSV). Amidst the distressing pessimism of the postmodern world, Christian faith formation offers hope to all people: oppressed and oppressors, poor and rich, weak and strong. Faith formation into an authentic Christianity reminds us that we are not alone. God, who has graciously forgiven

and liberated us, offers us hope that this is not the final chapter—
God has and will continue to redeem the world. This hope must be
central to faith formation in the postmodern matrix.

Questioning the "Right" Answers

*Faith formation in the postmodern matrix holds fast to the narrative
of God.* The postmodern world recognizes that human beings live
by narratives that are held and professed by their communities.
Thus, as I have alluded throughout this chapter, faith formation in
a postmodern world should be grounded on the narrative that the
Christian community professes as their true narrative: the story of
God. Yet while we believe that this story is true, we must admit that
our interpretations and articulations of it are not a complete and
inerrant representation of it, for "now we see in a mirror, dimly, but
them we will see face to face" (1 Cor. 13:12, NRSV).

Furthermore, if we really hold this story as true, then we should live
it out in our daily lives, for we are a part of it. The narrative of God
did not just happen a long time ago in a place far, far away. It began
before the creation of the world and is continuing today. It is, as
Brian McLaren says, "The story we find ourselves in."[43] Each of us is
part of this narrative, so we should live as though this is true. Faith
formation can help people to live into the narrative of God, to help
that story become their story. In the words of Walter Brueggemann,
"Our hope is that [people] will grow to affirm that this is my story
about me, and it is our story about us."[44]

Our affirmation of the truth of the narrative of God for the Christian
community makes sense in a postmodern world. Yet in a paradoxical
way, it also challenges the postmodern view that anything goes when
it comes to narratives, that any narrative can be relatively true. The
story of God—as a story of love, justice, and peace—involves an
ethical imperative that challenges stories of violence, oppression,
and hatred.

Faith formation in a postmodern world, then, is not about cognitive
knowledge, proving others wrong and ourselves right, or growing
churches. It is about living into the story of God. When we find
ourselves a part of this narrative that we hold to be true, our actions

profess and are grounded in its truth. Alasdair McIntyre has written, "I can only answer the question 'What am I to do?' if I can answer the prior question 'Of what story or stories do I find myself a part?'"[45] Christians know what to do when we see ourselves as part of God's story. And when we live into this story through acts of love, justice, and peace, we become a city on a hill that graciously welcomes others to become a part of this story, to make it their story, and to help us write the story together. When we do all of this, we can have faith that moves mountains, faith that can change the world. But we mustn't forget to always rely on a healthy dose of grace.

Ending with a Starting Point

Let me end this chapter with a word about where we ought to begin faith formation. One of the problems with the modern church, I believe, is that it does not see how much of the Christian faith has been compromised to fit into a modern worldview. I hope that we in the postmodern world do not make the same mistake. As we think about the current and future shapes of faith formation, we ought to keep in mind that modernism is not the starting point, nor is postmodernism. Christ alone is our starting point, the solid rock on which our faith is grounded. Faith formation amidst a postmodern world is not about forming good modernists or about forming good postmodernists. It is, and always has been, about forming good Christians—followers of the risen Christ who hold the story of God as true for their communities. Let us always seek to form good story-tellers, story-keepers, and story-livers.

Conclusion:

The People
of the Story
of God's
Faithfulness

Robert J. Keeley

My children tease me about getting into ruts. Here's an example: I can take two different roads to get to our home from the campus where I teach. Once when I was driving with my youngest daughter I said, "Do you know why I go this way?" Her answer was immediate: "Because this is the way you go." They think I get a particular way of doing things and just keep doing that because I get in ruts. I claim they're overgeneralizing but the vote is unanimous—even my wife agrees with them.

My oldest daughter, who is twenty-six, got the game "Settlers of Catan" for Christmas. She had been a fan of the game for a while and had played it with friends, so she was glad to get her own copy. She taught me how to play it and said that she'd leave it at our house for a while so I could use it whenever I wanted to. This is a game with lots of pieces and parts to it, so setting it up takes a few minutes. I noticed that she was very particular in the way she put the game away, wanting to make sure that it was ready to be used the next time. A few days later she asked if I had played it without her yet and I mentioned that I was a little nervous about using it because I didn't want to put it away wrong. She said, "You know, Dad, I do it that way because of you." For years she had been with me as I carefully put my CDs or DVDs or games away and that had rubbed off on her. The way that I do things had an impact on the way she now does things.

Faith formation is a lot like that. The things we do with our children and with each other matter. In the previous twelve chapters we've explored faith formation from a number of different perspectives. As I read these chapters some common themes emerged—ideas that seem to resonate with many of the authors who contributed to this book. Even though the authors represent different Christian traditions, there are many things that we share in our thinking about faith formation. Here are some of the things that I heard as I read:

We need each other. We were created to live in community. Our faith is nurtured and grows as we interact with others. Hearing about and seeing the faith of our brothers and sisters in Christ encourages us and helps us. We need to be with each other, young and old, and we need to talk about how we see God working in our lives and in the lives of those around us. The church has a vital role in the development of the faith of all of us.

Faith begins in practice. We are embodied people. We are what we do. Cultivating habits that bring us into the presence of God is an important part of our faith formation. Many of these practices connect us to the ancient church—things like prayer and attending worship—but they are powerful ways of training ourselves to be more Christlike.

We are people of the story. The grand story of God's faithfulness to his people is also our story. We need to tell it often and tell it well. We need to tell it in our worship, in our celebration of the sacraments, and in all parts of our lives. There are many competing stories in our culture that are vying for prominence, so we need to make sure that the story of God and God's people is in our hearts and on our lips.

Worship has a special place in faith formation. Of all the faith practices, gathering together with other people of faith in worship is especially important. Praise, confession, the Word, receiving God's blessing, and the sacraments are vital ingredients in the life of faith. These liturgical elements shape us in profound ways.

Parents are important. It is hard to overestimate the importance of parents and the home environment in the nurture of children's faith. From our parents we get our foundational ideas of what faith is all about. The church needs to equip parents to nurture the faith of their children at home so they know that faith is not something that only happens at church.

Culture changes, God's Word remains relevant. As Christians we have a responsibility to have our finger on the pulse of culture so that we can continue to speak the language of the culture we live in. God's message does not change but the world does. We have a responsibility to help people see how God's Word connects to their world and stands in contrast to it.

Faith formation is a lifelong process. No matter how you look at it, faith formation is a lifetime event. It is not only children whose faith needs nurturing—all of us need it. Faith formation is an ongoing process that is lived out in the community of faith together with all God's people.

God's faithfulness is at the core of what we do. All of our work is nothing without the Holy Spirit working in our hearts and in the hearts of those around us. There is no single way to build faith in our congregations or in our families. The ideas presented in this book, however, give us a good starting point. We have a powerful God who goes before us and challenges us to walk in his ways. We are and continue to be the people of the story of God's faithfulness.

Contributors

Holly Catterton Allen is Professor of Christian Ministries and Director of the Child & Family Studies Program at John Brown University in Siloam Springs, Arkansas. She is the editor of *Nurturing Children's Spirituality: Christian Perspectives and Best Practices* (Cascade, 2008).

Sarah Arthur is a writer, speaker, and recent graduate of Duke Divinity School presently living in Lansing, Michigan. A former fulltime youth director, she is the author of *Walking with Frodo: A Devotional Journey through "The Lord of the Rings"* (Tyndale, 2003) and *The God-Hungry Imagination: The Art of Storytelling for Postmodern Youth Ministry* (Upper Room Books, 2007).

Timothy Brown is President and Henry Bast Professor of Preaching at Western Theological Seminary in Holland, Michigan. He is also the author of *Witness Among Friends* (CRC Publications, 1989) and *Let's Preach Together* (CRC Publications), as well as a contributing author in *The Church for All Ages* (Alban, 2008).

Elizabeth F. Caldwell is Associate Dean for Advising and Formation and the Harold Blake Walker Professor of Pastoral Theology at McCormick Theological Seminary. She is author of *Making a Home for Faith: Nurturing the Spiritual Life of Your Children* (United Church Press, 2007), *The Shelter, Nurture and Spiritual Fellowship of God's Children* (Geneva, 2006), and *Leaving Home with Faith: Nurturing the Spiritual Life of our Youth* (United Church Press, 2003).

Erik W. Carter is Associate Professor in the Department of Rehabilitation Psychology & Special Education at the University of Wisconsin-Madison. He is the author of *Including People with Disabilities in Faith Communities: A Guide for Service Providers, Families, & Congregations* (Paul H. Brookes Publishing Co., 2007).

Robbie Fox Castleman is Associate Professor of Biblical Studies and Theology at John Brown University in Siloam Springs, Arkansas. She is the author of *True Love in a World of False Hope* (InterVarsity

Press, 1996), *Faith on the Edge* (InterVarsity Press, 1999), and *Parenting in the Pew* (InterVarsity Press, 2002).

David M. Csinos recently completed a Th.M. in Christian Education at Union Theological Seminary and Presbyterian School of Christian Education in Richmond, Virginia. In addition to his academic pursuits, he has been a staff member in children's ministry in a number of churches in southern Ontario, Canada.

Fred P. Edie is Assistant Professor of the Practice of Christian Education at Duke Divinity School and Director of the Duke Youth Academy for Christian Formation. He is the author of *Book, Bath, Table, and Time: Christian Worship as Source and Resource for Youth Ministry* (Pilgrim, 2007).

Syd Hielema is the Chaplain and Associate Professor of Religion at Redeemer University College in Ancaster, Ontario. He is a member of the Faith Formation Committee for the Christian Reformed Church in North America and is the author of a number of articles on faith nurture.

Robert J. Keeley is Professor of Education and Chair of the Education Department at Calvin College in Grand Rapids, Michigan. He is the author of *Helping Our Children Grow in Faith* (Baker, 2008) and coauthor of *Celebrating the Milestones of Faith* (Faith Alive Christian Resources, 2009).

Kevin E. Lawson is Director of the Ph.D. and Ed.D. programs in Educational Studies at Talbot School of Theology, Biola University, in La Mirada, California. He is author of *How to Thrive in Associate Staff Ministry* (Alban, 2000) and serves as editor of the *Christian Education Journal*.

Marian Plant currently serves as Associate Professor and Schauffler Chair of Christian Education at Defiance College in Defiance, Ohio. She is the author of *Faith Formation in Vital Congregations* (Pilgrim, 2009).

Don C. Richter is the Associate Director of the Valparaiso Project on the Education and Formation of People in Faith. He coedited *Way to Live: Christian Practices for Teens* (Upper Room Books, 2002) and is the author of *Mission Trips That Matter: Embodied Faith for the Sake of the World* (Upper Room Books, 2008).

Endnotes

Chapter 2

[1] Craig Dykstra, *Growing in the Life of Faith*, second edition (Westminster John Knox, 2005), 66.

[2] C. Ellis Nelson, *Where Faith Begins* (John Knox, 1967).

[3] The early church understood the significance of practices in shaping faith for adult converts. Catechumens were trained and initiated into Christian faith through a three-year process of daily instruction. This training involved specific practices such as prayer, fasting, and resisting military conscription as they prepared "to put on Christ" in baptism. Mystagogy, a period of intense instruction for the newly baptized, signaled the need for fledgling disciples to continue lifelong learning in faith. This post-initiation training honored the mystery of sacramental faith, emphasizing that right Christian belief must be rooted in right worship (*lex orandi, lex credendi*). See Gordon Mikoski, *Baptism and Christian Identity: Teaching in the Triune Name* (Eerdmans, 2009).

[4] Howard Gardner, *Frames of Mind: The Theory of Multiple Intelligences* (Basic Books, 1983).

[5] Malcolm Gladwell, *Outliers* (Little, Brown & Company, 2008), 38-40.

[6] Prayer logic reflects the simple elegance of holophrastic speech, in which one word conveys a world of meaning: "mama/dada/abba" (adoration), "sorry" (confession), "why?" (lament), "help" (petition), "thanks" (thanksgiving)—see www.calvin.edu/worship/habits.

[7] *Practicing Theology*, edited by Miroslav Volf and Dorothy C. Bass (Eerdmans, 2002), 256.

[8] Ibid., 248-249.

[9] Ibid., 256.

[10] Dietrich Bonhoeffer wrote a doctoral thesis (*Sanctorum Communio*) advocating an understanding of Christian community that surpassed anything he himself had experienced in German parish life. Several years later, Bonhoeffer encountered the kind of church he had anticipated while worshiping at Abyssinian Baptist Church in Harlem. The church's Great Tradition shaped Bonhoeffer's beliefs even in the absence of vital practices. Then a congregation's vital practices confirmed his beliefs and encouraged him to strengthen the Christian practices of other communities upon return to his homeland. See Charles Marsh, "From the Phraseological to the Real: Lived Theology and the Mysteries of Practice" in the practicingourfaith.org library.

[11] In his introductory essay to *The School of Faith: The Catechisms of the Reformed Faith* (James Clarke & Co. Ltd., 1959), T. F. Torrance comments on how Luther's and Calvin's catechisms provide conceptual scaffolding that enable disciples to "reach beyond their grasp so that one day they might grasp beyond their initial reach." The subtitle of Thomas Long's book *Testimony* is "Talking Ourselves into Being Christian."

[12] See Patrick Miller, *The Ten Commandments* (Westminster John Knox, 2009), 415-432.

[13] Reading Acts 2, some identify five forms of ministry that have shaped the course of the church's life throughout the centuries: fellowship (*koinonia*), worship (*leiturgia*), teaching (*didache*), proclamation (*kerygma*), and service (*diakonia*). See James D. Smart, *The Rebirth of Ministry* (Westminster Press, 1960); and Maria Harris, *Fashion Me a People* (Westminster John Knox, 1989).

[14] This phrase is from Dorothy C. Bass and Susan R. Briehl, eds., *On Our Way: Christian Practices for Living a Whole Life* (Upper Room, 2010), 8. A more formal definition of Christian practices: things Christian people do together over time to address fundamental needs and conditions of humanity and all creation in the light of and in response to God's active presence for the life of the world in Jesus Christ. Dorothy C. Bass, ed., *Practicing Our Faith: A Way of*

Life for a Searching People, Revised 2nd Edition (Jossey-Bass, 2010), 204.

[15] In modern usage, the phrase "pearls of wisdom" refers to pithy sayings that can be bestowed on others. To the extent that wisdom entails patient observation over time, it's misleading to suggest that personal, hard-won insight can simply be handed over as one might hand someone a strand of pearls. The biblical book of Proverbs, which seems to dispense polished "pearls of wisdom" aplenty, actually presents a more nuanced and complex understanding of how wisdom shapes the moral imagination. See Christine Roy Yoder, *Proverbs* (Abingdon, 2009).

[16] This congregation reads *Making Room* by Christine Pohl (Eerdmans, 1999) and uses the companion study guide available at www.practicing ourfaith.org/cfm/library/pdf/MakingRoomStudyGuide.pdf.

[17] Christian Smith, *Souls in Transition* (Oxford University Press, 2009), 279-299.

[18] Camp Johnsonburg (campjburg.org) and Chestnut Ridge Camp and Conference Center (campchestnutridge.org) intentionally pattern their outdoor ministries in relation to Christian practices.

[19] The New Monasticism movement (newmonastism.org) fosters such households.

[20] Shades of Praise (shadesofpraise.org), an interracial gospel choir in New Orleans, became a lifeline after Hurricane Katrina.

[21] Living Waters for the World (livingwatersfortheworld.org) is an initiative of the Presbyterian Church (USA).

[22] LaSalle Street Church (Chicago) hosts "Breaking Bread"—see www.lasallestreetchurch.org/pages/serving/breakingbread.php.

[23] *Practicing Our Faith*, xvi.

[24] *Practicing Theology*, 254.

[25] Dykstra, op. cit.

Chapter 3

[1] Collier Books, Macmillan Publishing Company, 1952, 1970.

[2] Ibid., 71.

[3] Ibid., 85.

[4] All Scripture quotations in this chapter are from the New Revised Standard Version (Zondervan, 1991).

[5] See question 17 of the Westminster Shorter Catechism.

[6] See question 4 of the Westminster Shorter Catechism.

[7] See the entry for "gospel" in the *Concise Oxford English Dictionary*, eleventh edition (Oxford University Press, 2004).

[8] This "wondering" approach to religious education is articulated by Jerome Berryman in his "Godly Play" curriculum (see *Godly Play: An Imaginative Approach to Christian Education,* Augsburg, 1991). Godly play is based on the Montessori Method and was adapted for religious education by Bible scholar Sofia Cavalletti and her colleague Gianna Gobbi. For more information, see http://www. goodshepherdcatechesis.com/id1.html.

Chapter 4

[1] Caldwell, Elizabeth F., *Making a Home for Faith: Nurturing the Spiritual Life of Your Children* (Pilgrim Press, 2007), 7.

[2] Marty, Martin, "Christian Education in a Pluralist Culture" in *Rethinking Christian Education*, ed. David S. Schuller (Chalice Press, 1993), 22.

[3] Fitzpatrick, Jean Grasso, *Nurturing Your Child's Spiritual Growth* (Viking, 1991), 44.

[4] Miller-McLemore, Bonnie, *Let the Children Come: Reimagining Childhood from a Christian Perspective* (Jossey-Bass, 2003), 164-165.

[5] Dykstra, Craig, *Growing in the Life of Faith: Education and Christian Practices* (Geneva Press, 1999), 42-43.

[6] Gellman, Marc, and Thomas Hartman, *How Do You Spell God? Answers to the Big Questions from Around the World* (Morrow Junior Books, 1995), 145-146.

[7] Coles, Robert, *The Moral Intelligence of Children* (Random House, 1997), 31.

[8] Dykstra, 43.

[9] Wuthnow, Robert, *Growing Up Religious: Christians and Jews and their Journeys of Faith* (Beacon Press, 1999), xxxvi.

[10] Cahill, Lisa Sowle, *Family: A Christian Social Perspective* (Fortress Press, 2000), 137.

Chapter 5

[1] Fowler, James, *Stages of Faith* (Harper and Row, 1981).

[2] This comes from an understanding of Piaget's Theory of Cognitive Development.

[3] Read more about this in *Helping Our Children Grow in Faith* by Robert Keeley (Baker, 2008).

[4] Stokes, Kenneth, *Faith Is a Verb* (Twenty-Third Publications, 1989).

[5] Stokes, 19.

[6] Fowler, 186

[7] Smith, Christian with Melissa Lundquist Denton, *Soul Searching* (Oxford University Press, 2005), 133.

Chapter 7

[1] Since baptism and holy communion are the two sacraments common to most Christian denominations, I will focus exclusively upon them. Of course, some traditions practice more sacraments,

others fewer. In addition, some traditions prefer "Eucharist" ("thanksgiving") or "Lord's Supper" to "holy communion." For simplicity's sake I will stick to "holy communion" and intend it as broadly synonymous with the other terms, though alert readers will detect that the different names for the rite highlight different theological dimensions of it.

Chapter 8

[1] See Sondra Higgins Matthaei, "Rethinking Faith Formation" in *Religious Education* (Taylor & Francis, Inc., Winter 2004), 57, referring to Matthaei, *Making Disciples: Faith Formation in the Wesleyan Tradition* (Abingdon Press, 2000), 22.

[2] Based on concepts discussed by Myles Horton and Paulo Freire in the book *We Make the Road by Walking: Conversations on Education and Social Change*, ed. Brenda Bell, John Gaventa, and John Peters (Temple University Press, 1990).

Chapter 9

[1] Martineau, M., J. Weber, and L. Kehrwald, *Intergenerational Faith Formation: All Ages Learning Together* (Twenty-Third Publications, 2008); Meyers, P., *Live, Learn, Pass It On! The Practical Benefits of Generations Growing Together in Faith* (Discipleship Resources, 2006); Vanderwell, H. ed., *The Church of All Ages: Generations Worshiping Together* (Alban Institute, 2008).

[2] Passover (Ex. 12; 23:15; 34:18, 25; Lev. 23:5-8; Num. 9:1-14; 28:16-25; Deut. 16:1-8; Ezek. 45:21-24), the Feast of Weeks (Ex. 23:16; 34:22; Lev. 23:15-21; Num. 28:26-31; Deut. 16:9-10), the Feast of Booths (Ex. 23:16; 34:22; Lev. 23:33-36; Num. 28:12-39; Deut. 16:13-18), and the Feast of Trumpets (Lev. 23:23-25; Num. 29:1-6).

[3] For example, White, J., *Intergenerational Religious Education* (Religious Education Press, 1988); Stonehouse, C., *Joining Children on the Spiritual Journey: Nurturing a Life of Faith* (Baker Books, 1998); and Harkness, A. G., "Intergenerational and Homogeneous-age Education: Mutually Exclusive Strategies for Faith Communities?" (*Religious Education*, V. 95, Issue 1, 2000) 51-63.

[4] Allen, H. "A qualitative study exploring the similarities and differences of the spirituality of children in intergenerational and non-intergenerational Christian contexts." (Doctoral dissertation, Talbot School of Theology, Biola University, 2002.) *Dissertation Abstracts International, 63-04A.*

[5] For more information you can see Vygotsky, L. S., *Mind in Society: The Development of Higher Psychological Process,* M. Cole, V. John-Steiner, S. Scribner, & E. Souberman, eds. (Harvard University Press, 1978), (original works written in the 1920s and 1930s, published variously in 1930, 1935, 1956, 1960, and 1966) or Vygotsky, L. S., *Educational Psychology,* R. Silverman, trans., (St. Lucie Press, 1997), (original work published in 1926).

[6] Powell, K., "Is the Era of Age Segregation Over? An Interview with Kara Powell," *Leadership* 30, (3) Summer 2009, 43-48.

[7] Marr, P. R., "Development of an intergenerational curriculum for Christian education ministry in the church." (Doctoral dissertation, Eastern Baptist Theological Seminary, 1990.) *Dissertation Abstracts International, 51-04A.*

[8] White, J., *Intergenerational Religious Education.*

[9] Marr, 201.

[10] Chesto, K. O. "FIRE (Family-centered intergenerational religious education): An alternative model of religious education." (D. Min. dissertation, Hartford Seminary, 1987.) *Dissertation Abstracts International, 48-08A,* 75.

[11] This refers to the work of Vygotsky, as noted earlier and also the work of Lave, J., & Wenger, E., *Situated learning: Legitimate peripheral participation,* (Cambridge University Press, 1991).

[12] Westerhoff III, J. H., *Will Our Children Have Faith?* (Seabury Press, 1976); Fowler, J. W., *Weaving the New Creation: Stages of Faith and the Public Church* (HarperCollins, 1991).

[13] Gambone, J., *All Are Welcome: A Primer for Intentional Intergenerational Ministry and Dialogue* (Elder Eye Press, 1998); Glassford, D., "Fostering an Intergenerational Culture," in H. Vanderwell, ed., *The Church of All Ages: Generations Worshiping Together* (Alban Institute, 2008); Prest, E., *From One Generation to Another* (Capetown, Training for Leadership, 1993); Rendle, G., "Intergenerational as a Way of Seeing," in. H. Vanderwell, ed., *The Church of All Ages: Generations Worshiping Together* (Alban Institute, 2008); White, J., *Intergenerational Religious Education.*

[14] Prest, 22.

[15] Lave & Wenger, 122.

Chapter 10

[1] Carter, E. W., *Including People with Disabilities in Faith Communities: A Guide for Service Providers, Families, and Congregations* (Paul H. Brookes, 2007).

[2] Some of this data may be found at provincial websites for Canada. Facts about British Columbia, for example, are found at http://www. bcstats.gov.bc.ca.

[3] Schultheiss, S., "Make It Matter: All Work, All Play," *Readers Digest* (September 2009), 44.

[4] Reinders, H. S., *Receiving the Gift of Friendship: Profound Disability, Theological Anthropology, and Ethics* (Eerdmans, 2008).

[5] Gaventa, W., "Religious Ministries and Services with Adults with Developmental Disabilities," in J. A. Summers, ed., *The Right to Grow Up: An Introduction to Adults with Developmental Disabilities* (Paul H. Brookes, 1985), 191-226.

Chapter 11

[1] Coles, Robert, *The Spiritual Life of Children* (Mariner Books, 1991).

[2] Hay, David and Rebecca Nye, *The Spirit of the Child* (Jessica Kingsley, 1998).

[3] Wuthnow, Robert, *Growing Up Religious: Christians and Jews and Their Journeys of Faith* (Beacon Press, 1999).

[4] Hyde, Brendan, *Children and Spirituality* (Jessica Kingsley, 2008).

[5] Westerhoff, John, *Will Our Children Have Faith?* (Morehouse, 2000).

[6] Smith, Christian and Melina Lundquist Denton, *Soul Searching* (Oxford University Press, 2009).

[7] Roehlkepartain, Eugene, *The Teaching Church* (Abingdon Press, 1993).

[8] Black, Wesley, "Stopping the Dropouts: Guiding Adolescents Toward a Lasting Faith Following High School Graduation," *Christian Education Journal*, V. 5, No. 1 (Spring 2008), 28-46.

[9] Fowler, James, *Stages of Faith* (HarperSanFrancisco, 1995).

[10] Knowles, Malcolm et.al., *The Adult Learner* (Amsterdam: Elsevier, 2005).

[11] Cross, K., *Adults as Learners: Increasing Participation and Facilitating Learning* (Jossey-Bass, 1992).

[12] Wuthnow, Robert, *Sharing the Journey* (Free Press, 1996).

[13] Hawkins, Greg and Cally Parkinson, *Reveal: Where Are You* (Willow Creek Association, 2007) and Hawkins, Greg and Cally Parkinson, *Follow Me* (Willow Creek Resources, 2008).

[14] Hagberg, Janet, *The Critical Journey, Stages in the Life of Faith*, 2nd edition (Sheffield Publishing, 2004).

Chapter 12

[1] My use of the word *modern* in this chapter must not be confused with those who use the term to describe the contemporary world. When I refer to the *modern era* or *modernism*, I speak of the time period in the West that consisted of roughly the past 400 or 500 years, which was characterized by an emphasis on reason.

[2] There are several excellent texts that take a more in-depth look at postmodernism and the implications of the movement for the contemporary church. Readers seeking more depth and breadth on this subject should investigate Stanley J. Grenz, *A Primer on Postmodernism* (Eerdmans, 1996); Brian D. McLaren, *A Generous Orthodoxy* (Zondervan, 2004); Brian D. McLaren, *A New Kind of Christian: A Tale of Two Friends on a Spiritual Journey* (Jossey-Bass, 2001); J. Richard Middleton and Brian J. Walsh, *Truth Is Stranger Than It Used to Be: Biblical Faith in a Postmodern Age* (InterVarsity Press, 1995); Carl Raschke, *The Next Reformation: Why Evangelicals Must Embrace Postmodernity* (Baker Academic, 2004); Phyllis Tickle, *The Great Emergence: How Christianity Is Changing and Why* (Baker, 2008); and Baker Academic's The Church and Postmodern Culture series: James K. A. Smith, *Who's Afraid of Postmodernism? Taking Derrida, Lyotard, and Foucault to Church* (2006); John D. Caputo, *What Would Jesus Deconstruct? The Good News of Postmodernism for the Church* (2007); and Carl Raschke, *GloboChrist: The Great Commission Takes a Postmodern Turn* (2008).

[3] Walsh, Brian J. and Sylvia C. Keesmaat, *Colossians Remixed: Subverting the Empire* (InterVarsity, 2004), 22.

[4] Smith, James K. A., *Who's Afraid of Postmodernism? Taking Derrida, Lyotard, and Foucault to Church.*

[5] Smith, 56.

[6] Grenz, Stanley J., *A Primer on Postmodernism* (Eerdmans, 1996).

[7] Moore's documentaries include *Sicko* (2007), *Bowling for Columbine* (2002), *The Big One* (1997), and *Roger and Me* (1989).

[8] Grenz, 20.

[9] Rogoff, Barbara, *The Cultural Nature of Human Development* (Oxford University Press, 2003), 368.

[10] Grenz, 20 and 25.

[11] Bragg, Melvyn and Norman Jewison. *Jesus Christ Superstar*. DVD. Directed by Norman Jewison. Hollywood: Universal Pictures, 1973.

[12] Jones, Tony, "(De)Constructing Justice: What Does the Postmodern Turn Contribute to the Christian Passion for Justice?" in *The Justice Project*, ed. Brian McLaren, Elisa Padilla, and Ashley Bunting Seeber, 58-63 (Baker, 2009), 61.

[13] Grenz, 7.

[14] Grenz, 40-41.

[15] Grenz, 43.

[16] Grenz, 8 and 14.

[17] Even this modified version of Pilate's question is insufficient, because the English language lacks a plural second-person pronoun. Perhaps we can employ southern dialect to better reflect the postmodern view of communal truth: "What are truths? Are ours the same as y'all's?"

[18] Birns, Nicholas, "Deconstruction," in *Encyclopedia of Postmodernism*: 84-6, 85.

[19] McLaren, Brian D., *A New Kind of Christianity: Ten Questions That Are Transforming the Faith* (HarperOne, 2010), 55.

[20] Middleton, J. Richard and Brian J. Walsh, *Truth Is Stranger Than It Used to Be: Biblical Faith in a Postmodern Age* (InterVarsity, 1995).

[21] Middleton and Walsh, 33.

[22] Grenz, 148.

[23] Smith, 34.

[24] Smith, 37.

[25] Derrida, Jacques. *Of Grammatology*, trans. G. Spivak (Johns Hopkins University Press, 1976), 158.

[26] Smith, 39.

[27] Smith, 44.

[28] Bartholomew, Craig G. and Michael W. Goheen, *The Drama of Scripture: Finding Our Place in the Biblical Story* (Baker Academic, 2004), 18.

[29] Smith, 65.

[30] Lyotard, Jean-François, *The Postmodern Condition: A Report on Knowledge*, trans. G. Bennington and B. Massumi (University of Minnesota Press, 1984), xxiv.

[31] Smith, 66.

[32] Smith, 69.

[33] Lyotard, 8.

[34] Smith, 125.

[35] Csinos, David M., Daniel L. Jennings, Brian D. McLaren, and Karen Marie Yust, "Where Are the Children? Keeping Sight of Young Disciples in the Emerging Church Movement," *The Journal of Family and Community Ministries: Empowering Through Faith* 23:4 (2010).

[36] Grenz, 19.

[37] Densham, Pen, *Robin Hood: Prince of Thieves*. DVD. Directed by Kevin Reynolds (Warner Bros. Pictures, 1991).

[38] Robertson, Roland, "Globalization and the Future of 'Traditional Religion,'" in *God and Globalization, Vol. 1: Religion and the Powers of the Common Life*, ed. Max L. Stackhouse with Peter J. Paris, 53-68 (T&T Clark, 2000), 64.

[39] Grenz, 29.

[40] There has been a great deal of recent writing on the topic of spiritual practices. Readers would do well to investigate Richard J. Foster,

Celebration of Discipline: The Path to Spiritual Growth (Harper, 1998); Dallas Willard, *The Spirit of the Disciplines: Understanding How God Changes Lives* (HarperSanFrancisco, 1988); Valerie E. Hess, *Spiritual Discipline's Devotional: A Year of Readings* (InterVarsity, 2007); Tony Jones, *The Sacred Way: Spiritual Practices for Everyday Life* (Zondervan, 2005); Dorothy C. Bass, ed., *Practicing our Faith: A Way of Life for a Searching People* (Jossey-Bass, 1997); and Brian McLaren, *Finding Our Way Again: The Return of the Ancient Practices* (Thomas Nelson, 2008). Notable series on spiritual practices are the Practices of Faith Series (edited by Dorothy C. Bass and published by Jossey-Bass) and The Ancient Practices Series (edited by Phyllis Tickle and published by Thomas Nelson).

[41] Freire, Paolo, *Pedagogy of the Oppressed*, trans. Myra Bergman Ramos (Herder and Herder, 1970).

[42] Grenz, 7.

[43] McLaren, Brian D., *The Story We Find Ourselves In: Further Adventures of a New Kind of Christian* (Jossey-Bass, 2003).

[44] Brueggemann, Walter, *Belonging and Growing in the Christian Community* (General Assembly Mission Board, Presbyterian Church in the United States, 1979), 31.

[45] MacIntyre, Alasdair, *After Virtue*, third edition (University of Notre Dame Press, 2007), 216.